Safe or Secure?

Safe or Secure? examines the evolution and deployment of age verification systems, situating them within broader technological, regulatory, and societal frameworks. It analyzes this trend as part of the international response to the rapid expansion of the internet and subsequent exposure of minors to online content that was not originally designed with age-based boundaries.

Drawing on developments across the globe, the book traces how age verification has progressed from simple offline age checks to cutting-edge solutions embedded within online services and digital platforms. It explores the persistent tension between child protection objectives and the need to safeguard privacy and data rights, a balance that continues to shape regulatory decisions and system design. The discussion covers a range of approaches currently in use or under development, including identity document verification, financial and institutional linkages, and emerging biometric and behavioral techniques such as facial analysis, voice, and electrocardiogram. These developments are examined in relation to their practical deployment, limitations, and implications for governance. The book also covers ongoing debate over where age verification should be implemented across the digital stack—at the device, operating system, app store, or platform level—and how this reflects unresolved questions of responsibility and accountability among different players of the ecosystem.

Structured to provide a clear progression from historical foundations to contemporary practice, the book is organized into thematic chapters and is written to remain accessible to readers across disciplines, including policymakers, engineers, researchers, practitioners, as well as broader stakeholders such as activists, educators, parents, and general users engaged in the ongoing discourse on online safety and digital governance.

Azfar Adib is a doctoral researcher in Electrical and Computer Engineering at Concordia University, Canada. His research and advocacy include privacy-preserving approaches to age verification for safer online environments. He brings together a versatile portfolio in writing, public speaking, and leadership focused on technology, policy, and youth empowerment, supported by professional experience in telecommunications, academic training in both business and engineering, and extensive community engagement across Bangladesh and Canada.

Safe or Secure?

Decoding Age Verification in the Digital Era

Azfar Adib

CRC Press
Taylor & Francis Group
Boca Raton London New York

CRC Press is an imprint of the
Taylor & Francis Group, an **informa** business

Designed cover image: Shutterstock

First edition published 2027
by CRC Press
2385 NW Executive Center Drive, Suite 320, Boca Raton FL 33431

and by CRC Press
4 Park Square, Milton Park, Abingdon, Oxon, OX14 4RN

CRC Press is an imprint of Taylor & Francis Group, LLC

ISBN: 978-1-041-08118-0 (hbk)
ISBN: 978-1-041-08053-4 (pbk)
ISBN: 978-1-003-64351-7 (ebk)

DOI: 10.1201/9781003643517

Typeset in Minion
by Deanta Global Publishing Services, Chennai, India

Contents

List of Figures

List of Tables

Preface

THE EMERGENCE OF THE internet in the early 1990s came with immense promise—the open flow of information and unprecedented access to digital platforms. Indeed, the world has been transformed by the internet. However, it has also become clear that not everything can remain entirely open and unregulated.

One of the most pressing challenges has been the exposure of minors to online content—particularly social media, video games, and adult content—often described as one of the largest uncontrolled experiments in human history. Ensuring a clear boundary between adults and minors has long been an expectation, yet only recently has this begun to take concrete form with the global rise of age verification systems. What was barely imaginable a decade ago has now become a defining feature of digital governance.

For example, just over the past year (2025–2026), the world has witnessed several major developments, including social media restrictions for under-16s in Australia and Indonesia, pornographic site restrictions for under-18s in the UK, and the progress of age-verification-related laws and legislation across several jurisdictions. These developments reflect a rapidly expanding global shift toward structured age verification frameworks.

However, reaching this stage has not been straightforward. The journey has involved continuous tension between two fundamental priorities: protecting children online and safeguarding privacy and data rights. This tension has shaped policy debates, regulatory approaches, and technological innovation. It has also led to the emergence of a new age verification industry and accelerated research. Now a variety of methods exist for age verification—ranging from identity document verification and financial linkage to biometric and behavioral signals such as facial images, voice, hand gestures, and online activity.

Age verification has evolved from rudimentary offline checks into a cornerstone of international digital child protection policy. It is now a multidimensional field: a growing industry, a site of continuous technological innovation, a subject of active social and political debate, and an area where regulatory frameworks and technical standards are rapidly taking shape.

This book is a modest attempt to capture the evolving landscape of age verification. It explores its technological, regulatory, and social dimensions, each of which deserves extensive and separate discussion. As such, the book is intended as an overview rather than a detailed treatment. The author does not claim to be an expert in all aspects of this rapidly evolving field, but rather presents insights drawn from his academic research, community engagement, and professional experience.

The book is written to be accessible to readers across domains, including industry, academia, government, civil society, regulators, policymakers, engineers, and social advocates, as well as general readers. The language has been kept as clear and non-technical as possible, except in Chapter 4 (Age Verification Standards) and Chapter 7 (the author's research on ECG-based age estimation and age verification), where some technical detail is unavoidable.

Structurally, the book traces the evolution of age verification from its origins to its integration into the modern digital environment. Chapters 1 and 2 examine its historical development, Chapter 3 focuses on regulation, Chapter 4 discusses standards, Chapter 5 reviews recent deployments, Chapter 6 explores methods, and Chapter 7 highlights how an age verification technology is researched at a fundamental level. The last chapter provides a chronological view of this evolving field.

While the author is engaged in research and advocacy in this area, a neutral, evidence-based approach has been maintained throughout. References to specific commercial providers or specific research have been avoided. Chapters 2 and 7 are mostly based on the author's own research and advocacy journey, but remain grounded in facts and documented findings.

Age verification is a highly dynamic field. Between the time of this manuscript writing (April 2026) and publication, further developments are certain to emerge. This continual evolution is precisely what makes the field both challenging and exciting.

Looking ahead, age verification will continue to evolve in unexpected ways, making it a fascinating field to follow.

Acknowledgments

I EXPRESS MY SINCERE GRATITUDE to Taylor & Francis Publications for entrusting me with this book on a topic of current interest. I am very thankful to the editorial team for their continuous guidance and patience—particularly Randi Slack and Poppy Knight.

As the author, my analysis in this book mostly draws upon my work as a PhD researcher in Electrical and Computer Engineering at Concordia University in Montréal, Canada, where I specialize in privacy-preserving age verification technologies. The work is further inspired by Montréal's growing movement advocating for stronger age verification measures to ensure online safety.

I am profoundly grateful to all who have guided and inspired me throughout this journey. It starts with Mr Pierre Beauregard, whom I met by chance at a university event in early 2020. He introduced me to the broader movement for child online protection, and over the years has remained my constant mentor. A big contributor to this movement is my friend Rafaela Lee, founder of the Stop Exploitation Hub. Her tireless dedication, often standing alone with a banner on the streets, deserves admiration.

I am grateful to Ms Penny Rankin, President of the National Council of Women of Canada. Her vision has always inspired me. My heartfelt thanks also go to my neighbor, Ms Franca Circelli, whose encouragement kept me moving.

I would like to acknowledge Senator Julie Miville-Dechêne, whose longstanding and relentless contributions to advancing age verification legislation in Canada have been a significant source of inspiration for many people.

My gratitude to my PhD supervisor, Professor Wei-Ping Zhu, for his impactful guidance and continuous support throughout my research.

One of my greatest inspirations is my late uncle, Brigadier (Retired) Dr Kalam Shashed, whose scholarly journey and ever-positive outlook on life continue to guide me. His entire family—my aunt Nasima Shahed, my cousins Anonna Shahed, Anna Smith, Ayon Shahed, Arpon Shahed, and my niece Nandini—has been a strong source of support throughout my years in Montreal.

Above all, I owe everything to my family—my mother, Dr Shamim Ara; my father, Dr Agha Masood Choudhury; my sister, Anushi Arvin; and my wife, Sabiha Rahman—whose love, patience, and belief in me continue to be my greatest motivation.

Disclaimers

THE AUTHOR WISHES TO state that, while this book is published as a commercial work, its content has been developed independently and is not influenced by any external commercial, academic, or policy-driven interests. All facts and figures presented are drawn from authentic sources and have been analyzed by the author with the utmost effort to maintain a neutral perspective.

One chapter includes the author's doctoral research (previously published in an academic journal and reproduced here in accordance with standard copyright practices) as an illustrative example of age verification research. Its inclusion is solely for academic reference and does not intend to promote this particular direction of research.

Foreword

THE QUESTION OF HOW to protect children online without undermining the rights and freedoms of adults has become one of the defining policy challenges of the digital age. Age verification, once a marginal and often ineffective concept, now sits at the center of this debate.

Azfar Adib's *Safe or Secure? Decoding Age Verification in the Digital Era* arrives at an important moment. As this book carefully sets out, age assurance has evolved from simple offline checks to a complex global ecosystem shaped by law, technology, and social expectations. Governments are moving from asking whether age checks are necessary to determining how they should be implemented, how effective they must be, and how privacy can be preserved in the process.

What distinguishes this work is its breadth and balance. It traces the historical foundations of age restrictions, examines the regulatory divergence across jurisdictions, and provides a clear account of the technical methods now available. It also recognizes the central tension that defines this field: the need to protect minors from harm while upholding fundamental rights, including their privacy and their access to lawful content.

From my perspective, working for the past eight years with age assurance technology providers globally, one of the most important contributions of this book is its emphasis on privacy-preserving approaches. The debate is often framed as a binary choice between safety and privacy. In reality, as both this research and the work of the industry demonstrate, well-designed systems can deliver both. The emergence of standards such as IEEE 2089.1 and ISO/IEC 27566-1 reflects a growing consensus that age assurance can be effective, proportionate, and respectful of users' data.

The book also arrives at a time when misconceptions are common. Age verification is frequently criticized on the basis of outdated assumptions about data collection or surveillance. In practice, modern solutions are increasingly based on data minimization, anonymization, and reusable credentials. At the same time, policymakers are rightly demanding higher levels of effectiveness, moving beyond self-declaration and inference toward systems that can be independently assessed and trusted.

There is, however, no single solution. As the author notes, the global landscape remains fragmented, with different jurisdictions adopting different legal and technical approaches. This diversity is likely to persist. What matters is that systems are interoperable, risk-proportionate, and subject to independent scrutiny. And we must learn the lessons of history in this field, albeit a short one, and apply those to any new silver-bullet proposals that may initially appeal but may have unintended consequences.

Ultimately, this is not just a technical or regulatory issue. It is about how society defines responsibility in the digital environment. Platforms that profit from high-risk content must play a central role in ensuring that children are protected. At the same time, users must be given choices, and markets must remain open to innovation.

This book provides a valuable guide to that rapidly evolving landscape. It will be of interest to policymakers, lawyers, technologists, and anyone seeking to understand how age assurance can be deployed in a way that is both effective and rights-respecting.

Iain Corby
Executive Director
Age Verification Providers Association (AVPA)

CHAPTER 1

The Origins of Age Verification

To understand how the concept of age verification emerged, it is necessary to begin with the origins of the minimum age requirement, commonly referred to as the age of majority.

1.1 THE AGE OF MAJORITY

The age of majority, the legal threshold at which individuals gain full adult rights and responsibilities, has deep roots across ancient religious scriptures, evolved through country-specific laws, and has been standardized globally by modern international conventions.

1.1.1 Religious Foundations

Across religious traditions, maturity is defined more by readiness for responsibility than by fixed numerical ages. Physical, moral, and spiritual development are key indicators of responsibility in religious, legal, and communal life.

DOI: 10.1201/9781003643517-1

In Judaism, religious responsibility begins at 13 with the bar mitzvah. Full civic and legal duties are often expected later in adolescence or adulthood. Biblical texts also assign roles such as civic, religious, and military service from age 20.

In Christianity, maturity is often associated with preparation and leadership. Jesus is traditionally understood to have begun his ministry around age 30, symbolizing adulthood and wisdom.

In Islam, maturity is linked to puberty. This marks the start of religious obligations such as prayer and fasting. Legal adulthood is often recognized later, commonly around 18.

Hindu traditions describe gradual stages of responsibility. These can begin in childhood and progress through education, marriage, and social roles toward adulthood.

In Buddhism, readiness is prioritized over age. Early novice ordination is possible, but full monastic status is typically reserved for adults, often around age 20. Sikhism similarly emphasizes moral maturity and knowledge over strict age thresholds.

Across these traditions, a common pattern emerges. Age is used as a practical marker of maturity. It helps determine when individuals are ready to assume adult responsibilities [1–5].

1.1.2 From Magna Carta to Colonial Legacy—Britain's Majority Age of 21

By the 13th century, English common law set 21 as the age of majority. This originated in the Magna Carta (1215), which protected heirs under 21 from early marriage or exploitation. It also reflected the completion of knightly training—usually 21 years for full knights. By Edward I's reign (1272–1307), laws like the Statute of Westminster formalized it. Minors under 21 could not hold land, marry without consent, or make binding contracts.

As Britain expanded its colonial influence, the English common law shaped legal systems in many territories, although adoption varied by region and context. In the American colonies, the age of 21 was inherited from the English common law. After independence, most US states continued to use 21 for key rights such as voting, military eligibility, and alcohol access until major reforms in 1971, when the voting age was lowered to 18. The legal drinking age, however, remains 21. In Canada, the age of majority was commonly 21 under provincial law and was gradually reduced to 18 or 19 during the 1970s. In India, the legal framework under the Indian Majority Act 1875 generally established adulthood at 18, although certain guardianship and legal responsibilities extended to 21 in specific cases. After independence in 1947, India largely retained 18 as the standard age of majority. Some African countries maintained for a long time the British concept of 21 years, though most countries now use 18 as the standard age of majority [6–9].

1.1.3 Changing Age Norms in the Modern Era

World Wars I and II created major pressure on age limits through mass conscription. In World War I, Britain and the US drafted men starting at 18, sending teenagers to the frontlines while still denying them full civic rights like voting, which remained at 21. World War II expanded the scale: the US drafted men aged 18–45, while the UK drafted 18–41. Millions of young adults faced combat, yet they could not vote or enter binding contracts. This led to the rallying cry "old enough to fight, old enough to vote," a slogan that resurfaced during the Vietnam War in the 1960s.

Despite these pressures, all the US states kept 21 as the legal age of majority till 1970, regulating voting, contracts, and alcohol sales. The disconnect between military service and civil rights became politically charged during the Vietnam War, when 18-year-olds were drafted into combat but barred from voting. In response, Congress proposed and rapidly ratified the 26th Amendment in 1971, lowering the voting age to 18. By 1975, most US states aligned other adult rights, such as contract and legal emancipation, with 18, while alcohol consumption bar largely remained at 21 under federal incentives [10, 11].

Wars and industrialization gradually lowered age limits around the world. In the UK, the Family Law Reform Act 1969 (effective 1970) lowered the age of majority from 21 to 18. France did the same with Civil Code reforms in 1974, and Japan revised its Civil Code pretty recently in 2022 under the Reiwa reforms, lowering the age of majority from 20 to 18 [12–14].

1.1.4 UN Convention and Global Standardization

The United Nations Convention on the Rights of the Child (UNCRC), adopted in 1989 and ratified by 196 countries, is the most widely supported human rights treaty in history. It defines a child as anyone under 18. This baseline ensures protection from exploitation, abuse, and discrimination, while allowing flexibility for cultural or legal contexts where maturity comes sooner, such as some tribal or customary systems. It requires states to protect children's rights in education, health, and justice, regardless of race, gender, or origin [15].

The UNCRC helped harmonize age standards globally and pressured countries like the United States (signed but not ratified) toward alignment. However, it does not enforce the concept of uniform age in any country, allowing local variations. For example, Yemen sets the majority at 15 for some rights, Scotland allows marriage at 16, and Cuba at 14 in special cases. Despite these variations, UN monitoring has driven over 50 amendments worldwide since 1990, balancing child protection with recognition of evolving maturity. In some countries it led to constitutional amendment—like Brazil (amended constitution in 1988) and South Africa (amended constitution in 1996). Table 1.1 compares the age of majority and the voting age across selected countries [16].

TABLE 1.1 Age of majority and age of voting by selected countries worldwide

Country	Age of majority	Age of voting
United States	18	18
United Kingdom	18	18
Canada	18/19	18
France	18	18
Germany	18	18
Japan	18	18
India	18	18
Saudi Arabia	18	18
Nigeria	21	18
South Africa	18	18
Brazil	18	16
Australia	18	18
Thailand	20	18
Yemen	15	18
Angola	18/21	18
Cuba	18	16
Madagascar	21	18
Scotland	18	16

1.2 AGE-RESTRICTED COMMODITIES

Age restrictions for alcohol, tobacco, gambling, casinos, and cannabis began in the 19th century, driven by moral reforms, public health concerns, and campaigns to protect youth from addiction and vice. Industrialization, wars, and scientific discoveries about brain development, along with the emergence of new substances, gradually shaped these rules. By the late 20th and early 21st centuries, most countries had standardized age limits between 18 and 21.

Alcohol restrictions began with temperance movements in the 18th century, which were concerned about youth drinking and its links to crime and poverty. In 1923, Britain introduced a law banning alcohol sales to those under 18. The United States later set 21 as the minimum drinking age. After a rise in traffic deaths, the National Minimum Drinking Age Act (1984) pushed all states to adopt 21 by 1988. Today, most countries set alcohol age limits between 18 and 21 [17–19].

Tobacco laws also started early in the United States, where even young children were reported to smoke in the late 1800s. By 1920, many states set the minimum purchase age at 21, though it later dropped to 18. Countries like the UK and France also adopted 18 as the standard age [20, 21].

Gambling restrictions developed due to concerns about organized crime and youth betting. In the United States, lotteries and bingo set minimum ages between 18 and 21 by the 1970s. European countries gradually set limits from 16 to 18. In Asia, Japan sets the age at 20 for activities like pachinko(a gambling game). Today, most online gambling platforms require users to be between 18 and 21 [22, 23].

Casino regulations were tied to high-risk gambling. In 1931, Nevada—home to Las Vegas—legalized casinos with a minimum age of 21, partly to prevent youth involvement in crime. By the 1990s, most US states followed this standard. Globally, places like Macau and Singapore require gamblers to be 21, while Monte Carlo allows access from 18, reflecting local policies [22, 23].

Cannabis laws are more recent. Early US rules had no clear age limits, but legalization—starting with medical use in California (1996) and recreational use in states like Colorado and Washington (2012)—led most states to set the minimum age at 21. Canada set it at 18 or 19 (depending on the province) after legalization in 2018, while Uruguay uses 18. Many European countries also follow 18. These limits are influenced by research on brain development and the effects of THC on young people [24].

1.3 THE INTERNET BOOM AND THE NEW ERA OF AGE VERIFICATION

The internet originated in the late 1960s with the creation of ARPANET, but it was during the 1990s that it truly transformed from a research tool into a global phenomenon. In 1990, Tim Berners-Lee invented the World Wide Web, introducing the first web browser and server, which made it possible to share and access information through web pages. The release of the Mosaic browser in 1993 brought a graphical interface to the web, making it accessible to everyday users and fueling rapid growth. By the mid-1990s, commercial internet service providers began offering connections to households, and the removal of restrictions on commercial use led to a wave of innovation, including the launch of popular websites and the rise of the dot-com boom. This period marked the beginning of the internet as we know it today—a decentralized, global network that revolutionized communication, commerce, and culture [25].

1.3.1 Children's Online Privacy Protection Act

The Children's Online Privacy Protection Act (COPPA) is a US federal law enacted in 1998 and effective from April 2000, designed to protect the privacy of children under the age of 13 online. The law applies to any service directed at children or any service that knows it is collecting personal data from children under 13, regardless of the operator's location, as long as the service is accessible to US children.

The need for this act arose from the rapid growth of the internet and digital technologies, which created new risks for children's privacy and safety online. Before COPPA, websites and apps could collect, use, and even sell children's personal information without any legal restrictions, exposing young users to potential harm such as identity theft, targeted advertising, and inappropriate content. Children often lack the maturity to understand privacy policies or recognize the risks of sharing personal information, making them especially vulnerable to exploitation and misuse of their data.

COPPA addressed these concerns by requiring operators to obtain verifiable parental consent before collecting any personal information from children under 13, ensuring that parents have control over what data is collected and how it is used. The law also mandated that operators provide clear privacy notices, limit data collection to what is necessary, and implement robust security measures to protect children's information [26].

Ultimately, the concept introduced by COPPA and its age threshold of 13 became the benchmark for online age verification in the decades that followed, influencing global standards and regulatory approaches to children's digital privacy.

1.3.2 The Rise of Social Media

Social media emerged in the late 1990s with platforms like SixDegrees (1997), which allowed users to create profiles and connect with friends, setting the stage for modern networking. The early 2000s saw the rise of Friendster (2002) and MySpace (2003), both of which popularized personalization and broadened access to social networking. LinkedIn also launched in 2003, focusing on professional connections and career development. Facebook, founded in 2004, began as a university network but expanded globally, gradually becoming the largest social networking platform in human history.

As smartphones and mobile apps became widespread, new platforms like Snapchat (2011) and TikTok (2016) emerged, emphasizing ephemeral messaging and short-form video content. Social media experienced explosive growth between 2010 and 2020, fundamentally reshaping how people connect and communicate worldwide. In 2010, Facebook had about 500 million active users, making it the dominant platform, while Twitter had surpassed 100 million users and was gaining traction rapidly. LinkedIn, launched in 2003, had established itself as the leading professional network, with tens of millions of users by 2010.

By 2020, the landscape had transformed dramatically. Facebook's monthly active users had surged to over 3 billion, YouTube reached 2.5 billion, and Instagram and Snapchat each had over 1 billion users. TikTok, launched in 2016, became one of the fastest-growing platforms, amassing more than 1.5 billion monthly active users by 2020. LinkedIn continued to grow, reaching nearly 930 million users, while newer platforms like Telegram and Discord also gained significant traction [27–29].

Most major social media platforms, including Facebook, Instagram, Snapchat, Discord, YouTube, and TikTok, have set a minimum age of 13 for their users, aligning with the COPPA standard to protect children's privacy and safety online. For LinkedIn and Telegram, the minimum age is 16 years. These age thresholds reflect both legal requirements and industry norms. However, for many years, compliance relied largely on self-declaration, with no robust age-verification mechanisms in place until more recent regulatory interventions [30].

1.3.3 From Underground to Mainstream: The Emergence of Adult Online Content

The history of adult online content is deeply intertwined with the evolution of the internet itself,

Once restricted to printed magazines, VHS tapes, and adult video stores, adult content was a niche market with limited accessibility and high barriers to entry. The advent of the internet in the 1990s began to change this landscape, as websites started offering digitized images and videos, but these were often low-quality and scattered across the web. As broadband connections became widespread in the early 2000s, the ability to stream and download high-quality video content improved dramatically, making adult material far more accessible to a global audience. Platforms like Pornhub, launched in 2007, revolutionized the industry by providing free, user-generated content, removing the need for expensive subscriptions or physical media.

The launch of Pornhub in Montreal (Canada) in 2007 by four Concordia University graduates—Stephane Manos, Ouissam Youssef, Feras Antoon, and Matt Keezer—marked a pivotal moment in the mainstreaming of adult content online. Before Pornhub, adult content was often restricted to paid subscription sites or distributed through physical media. Pornhub founders' vision was to create a free, user-driven platform modeled after YouTube, where anyone could upload and access videos. This approach democratized access to adult material and fueled rapid growth, with Pornhub reaching one million daily visits within seven months and surpassing 10 million daily visitors by 2010. By 2020, Pornhub had become the most visited adult website worldwide, recording over 3.5 billion visits per month and accounting for approximately 21% of all global traffic to adult sites. The average visitor spent about 10 minutes per session, with mobile visits making up roughly 80% of total traffic.

The expansion of Pornhub coincided with broader shifts in internet culture and technology. As broadband access became widespread and mobile devices proliferated, online adult content became more accessible than ever before. Pornhub's success inspired a wave of similar platforms. The company's growth was further accelerated in 2010 when it was acquired by German entrepreneur Fabian Thylmann, who consolidated Pornhub with other major adult sites under the Manwin (later MindGeek) umbrella, creating the world's largest online adult entertainment empire [31–33].

However, this rapid expansion soon triggered intense global backlash—overexploitation issues and especially minors' access—ultimately accelerating the widespread adoption of age verification systems.

CHAPTER 2

Digital Risks to Minors

Origins of Modern Age Checks

2.1 ONLINE ADULT CONTENT: SCANDAL AND CRISIS

The Children's Online Privacy Protection Act (COPPA), enacted in 1998, represented a pioneering effort to safeguard children from unchecked data collection by online services, mandating verifiable parental consent before gathering personal information from minors. While this framework curbed some predatory practices on kid-focused sites, its enforcement proved uneven and limited in scope, relying heavily on self-regulatory compliance. Social media, which boomed globally in the late 2000s, implemented a 13+ minimum age policy, often banning younger users outright through simple self-reported age checks that lacked robust verification.

Adult sites, commonly known as pornographic sites, operated largely unchecked. Without age gates or content moderation, these sites were allowing minors easy access to explicit

DOI: 10.1201/9781003643517-2

material. By the mid-2010s, concerns escalated over reports of grooming, exposure to pornography, and emerging abuse cases, foreshadowing the scandals that would later demand sophisticated age verification solutions.

Pornhub, launched in 2007 by what would later become MindGeek and then Aylo, quickly dominated the online adult space, drawing billions of monthly visits by 2013 and rivaling top global sites in bandwidth. Its user-driven "tube" model—allowing anyone to upload videos without verification—fueled explosive growth but also enabled a flood of illicit material, including child sexual abuse material (CSAM), revenge porn, rape footage, and sex-trafficking content. Shocking cases emerged, such as a 2019 incident where 58 videos of a trafficked 15-year-old were hosted and labeled a "verified model" [34, 35].

By the end of the 2010s, these issues ignited a wave of US lawsuits against Pornhub. A 2020 California class action by over 40 GirlsDoPorn victims accused the platform of knowingly profiting from coercive trafficking since 2009. Similar suits followed, including a 2021 Alabama case by more than 20,000 minors victimized since 2011. In a pivotal 2023 admission, Pornhub pled guilty, paying a $1.8 million fine. In 2025, the FTC imposed a $5 million penalty on Pornhub for deceptive safety claims and CSAM mishandling. [36, 37].

In late December 2020, a seminal New York Times investigation by Nicholas Kristof unveiled Pornhub's vast repository of user-generated videos, including child sexual abuse material, non-consensual rape footage, and sex-trafficking recordings. The report included victim testimonies, such as Rose Kalemba, whose 2009 assault footage persisted online for years despite repeated removal requests, accumulating over 400,000 views. It also documented Pornhub's substantial revenue generation through advertising and affiliate partnerships, undertaken with apparent disregard for victims' entreaties [38].

Within days of this report, Pornhub brought down more than 10 million unverified videos, constituting 80% of its collection. It also imposed restrictions confining uploads to vetted partners. However, the decisive intervention came from Visa and Mastercard through their financial leverage. On December 9, 2020, Mastercard suspended all transactions with Pornhub, citing audit findings of unlawful content. Visa promptly took the same action. These measures affected Pornhub subscriptions on a huge scale [39].

Montreal, home to Pornhub's international headquarters, emerged as a focal point for grassroots activism against online exploitation. Leading the charge was Arrêter Exploitation Hub, founded in 2020 by activist Rafaela Diaz-Byers Lee. The group organized unwavering weekly protests every Tuesday outside Pornhub's offices since early 2020, demanding protection of minors along with the complete removal of non-consensual content [40].

Complementing this were allied women's organizations, such as the Montreal Council of Women (MCW), which joined International Women's Day protests on March 8, 2020, outside Pornhub HQ, decrying child access to porn and calling for third-party age verification. MCW president Penny Rankin emphasized protecting "young brains, young hearts, and young souls." Nationally, the National Council of Women of Canada (NCWC) urged protections against irreparable harm to women and children from sites like Pornhub [41]. Collectively, these movements bridged street-level activism with policy advocacy and prompted consequent actions by the Canadian government (Figure 2.1).

2.2 ONLINE ADULT CONTENT: ENFORCING AGE VERIFICATION

In late 2020, following the *New York Times* "Children of Pornhub" exposé and survivor testimony, more than 70 Canadian parliamentarians—53 MPs and 20 Senators from

FIGURE 2.1 Protests outside pornhub (currently Aylo) headquarters in Montreal.

multiple parties—co-signed a letter to the Canadian Police Commissioner calling for a criminal investigation into Pornhub. They alleged that the company had hosted and profited from child sexual abuse material (CSAM) and non-consensual pornography, and had failed to report such material to the Canadian Centre for Child Protection (C3P) and to US authorities as required by law. This political pressure created the backdrop for formal committee inquiries and later legislative initiatives.

The House of Commons Standing Committee on Access to Information, Privacy and Ethics (ETHI) opened a study titled "Ensuring the Protection of Privacy and Reputation on Platforms such as Pornhub," in which Pornhub executives, survivors, child-protection experts, and advocacy groups testified. Pornhub announced, during the study in December 2020, that it was disabling roughly 9–10 million unverified videos and removing its download button for most content—changes that it framed as a shift to a "verified uploader" model. However, witnesses told ETHI that such steps were reactive, not proactive, and that even removed content often reappeared across other sites via cross-posting and downloads.

Survivors described years-long struggles to have videos taken down and noted that when Pornhub removed a video, thumbnails, tags, and usernames often remained visible, continuing the harm. Child protection organizations such as the Canadian Centre for Child Protection testified that they had detected clear CSAM on Pornhub platforms at least 193 times over three years. It also clarified that while Pornhub had registered voluntarily to report to its Cyber Tipline in March 2020, this did not constitute any formal "partnership," contradicting Pornhub's earlier claims.

ETHI's June 2021 report concluded that Pornhub had systematically failed to protect privacy and reputation, and that its claims of "every video being reviewed by human moderators" were not credible given the volume of content and limited moderation resources. The committee urged stronger criminal enforcement, mandatory reporting compliance, independent age verification, and consent mechanisms [42].

Subsequently, the issue migrated into Senate debates on age verification bills, most notably Bill S-203 (Protecting Young Persons from Exposure to Pornography Act) and later S-210. The Standing Senate Committee on Legal and Constitutional

Affairs heard evidence that Pornhub had previously proposed its own age-verification solution (AgeID), raising concerns that the same company accused of hosting CSAM might control national age-gating infrastructure. Privacy officials warned Senators that any age-verification scheme must minimize personal data collection and avoid allowing entities like Pornhub to amass sensitive identity information [43].

The parliamentary scrutiny resulted in multiple enforcement and regulatory moves. Public Safety Canada started reviewing potential criminal investigation avenues regarding Pornhub's handling of CSAM. In parallel, the Office of the Privacy Commissioner of Canada (OPC) opened its own investigation into its compliance with Canadian privacy laws.

The OPC's 2024 report found significant risks of harm from "image-based abuse" (non-consensual pornography) on Pornhub sites. It concluded that Pornhub's reliance on moderators and AI tools was insufficient to ensure meaningful consent. It also confirmed that Pornhub's December 2020 content purge coincided with public allegations of CSAM hosting and that the company provided no evidence the policy shift had been planned earlier [44].

Canada's Parliament comprises the elected House of Commons and the appointed Senate. Private members' bills such as S-210 and S-209, concerning age verification for sexually explicit online material, first originated in the Senate. Independent Senator Julie Miville-Dechêne sponsored both measures. These bills propose criminalizing online pornographic content to minors without effective age verification.

Bill S-210, formally "An Act to restrict young persons' online access to sexually explicit material," was introduced in the Senate in November 2021. It mandates standard age verification methods, including ID documents or biometrics, for pornographic sites. Courts may direct internet service providers to block non-compliant sites. Exceptions exist for artistic or educational content. Privacy protection will be ensured by user data deletion immediately after verification. The Senate approved it unanimously in April 2023. In the House of Commons, it passed second reading 189–133 in December 2023. However, its progress halted after the 2025 Federal Election in Canada [45].

As an alternative, Bill S-209 titled "An Act to restrict young persons online access to pornographic material," emerged in May 2025. The Senate of Canada approved this bill in April 2026 as a renewed legislative effort to mandate age verification for sexually explicit online material following earlier stalled bills [46].

Taken together, these actions reframed adult sites not simply as controversial platforms but as a big priority for child protection—and, consequently, for privacy-preserving age verification.

2.3 SOCIAL MEDIA: GROWING NEED FOR AGE VERIFICATION

The early internet of the 1990s, and the emergence of social media platforms in the 2000s, offered children unrestricted access. In response to the US Children's Online Privacy Protection Act (COPPA) of 1998, most social media sites responded with simple 13+ minimums based on self-reported birthdates. Minors routinely circumvented these by falsifying ages. Some surveys in the 2010s showed that many children were using social media. In Europe, 53% of children aged 9–16 had social media accounts, and in the United States, 59% of preteens were using Facebook. High-profile cases on platforms like Snapchat and Instagram exposed serious risks, including online predators, sextortion, cyberbullying, and harmful content [47, 48].

Several tragic events pushed governments to take action. In 2017, a UK teenager, Molly Russell, died by suicide after being repeatedly shown self-harm content on Instagram [49]. In 2021, Facebook whistleblower Frances Haugen revealed that company leaders knew social media was harming teen mental health but did little to fix it [50].

After strong evidence of harm and repeated platform failures to self-regulate, governments around the world started to act. Australia took the lead with the 2024 Online Safety Amendment Act. It banned children under 16 from having social media accounts on platforms like TikTok, Instagram, Snapchat, and Facebook. Companies must use age-checking tools such as facial age scans or government ID. A comprehensive trial was conducted, followed by the successful implementation of under-16 access restrictions on social media across Australia in December 2025 [51–53].

France passed the 2023 Parental Control Law, which requires parental approval for children under 15 to join social media. Platforms must verify consent using methods like ID uploads, small credit card payments, or biometrics. Companies that break the rules can face fines of up to €15 million or 5% of global revenue. A 2024 government review found that while about half of platforms complied at first, many children still found ways to fake their age [54].

In the United States, many states introduced similar laws. By mid-2025, 13 states—including Utah, Texas, and Arkansas—required parental controls, data protections, or age verification. Some went further: Florida banned accounts for children under 14 and requires parental consent for ages 14–15. Nebraska now requires third-party age checks for all users under 18, starting in 2026, with fines of up to $100,000 per day [55].

The UK's Online Safety Act came into force in July 2025. It requires strong age checks for platforms that host content related to pornography, self-harm, suicide, or eating disorders. These checks can include facial scans, ID cards, or credit cards. The regulator, Ofcom, can fine companies up to £18 million or 10% of global revenue [56].

Across the EU, the Digital Services Act (in force since 2024) requires large platforms like Meta and TikTok to better protect children online. In 2025, the European Parliament proposed even stricter rules, including a minimum age of 16 with mandatory age verification. Fines could reach 6% of global revenue of the non-compliant organization [57, 58].

Together, these laws show a major shift—age verification is no longer optional for social media. They have moved from simple "enter your age" systems to real, verified age checks—from early privacy protections like COPPA to today's biometric and ID-based methods.

2.4 GAMING AND GENERATIVE AI: NEW HORIZONS IN ONLINE AGE VERIFICATION

Online gaming has become a primary entertainment medium for many people, with 3.5 billion users worldwide [59]. However, child grooming concerns through online games are escalating. A 2023 study in the United States found that nearly 75% of young people aged 10–17 experienced some form of harassment while participating in online multiplayer games [60]. Canadian Centre for Child Protection's January 2026 report reveals extreme online violence targeting girls rising sharply, with 84% of 75 tracked child victims (mostly teens) facing coercive tactics like blackmail and threats in social/gaming environments [61, 62].

Roblox, a popular online gaming platform, rolled out facial recognition-based age verification in November 2025. The purpose was to allow users to safely chat with users of similar ages. For example, those verified as under 9 can only chat with players up to the age of 13. Players deemed to be 16 can chat with players between 13 and 20.

However, the deployment faced severe challenges—misclassifying 23-year-olds as teens, 10-year-olds as adults, and even failing to identify marker-drawn whiskers or celebrity photos. Verified accounts as kids were sold on e-commerce platforms for $3-$4 to let adults bypass restrictions. Meanwhile, many users refused verification through selfies due to privacy fears, crippling chat usage. Consequently, players who used the text chat function had dropped from an average of 85 percent to 36 percent [63].

Discord is a messaging platform highly popular with gamers. In September 2025, a security breach at a third-party support provider for age verification in Discord exposed data for roughly 70,000 users, including sensitive government ID photos used for age verification, emails, and, in some cases, billing information [64].

Age verification is also becoming important for generative AI tools. Platforms like Midjourney, DALL-E, and Character. AI can create explicit images or adult-style conversations if minors enter certain prompts. To reduce this risk, some companies now use stronger age checks.

For example, OpenAI's ChatGPT Plus (2025) introduced selfie-based age verification for adult content and deletes the image after the check [65]. Stability AI blocks users under 18 by using device data and behavior patterns, such as typing speed and the type of questions asked, to estimate age [66]. Character. AI faced lawsuits in 2024 after children accessed sexual role-play bots. In response, it added age gates that use voice verification when users sign up [67].

In Europe, the AI Act now treats some generative AI systems as "high risk" and requires strong protections for minors, such as verified parental consent or privacy-preserving age checks. In April 2026, the Liberal Party of Canada (in power since 2015) adopted a motion to restrict under-16 access to social media and generative AI. Following this, the Minister of Canadian Heritage emphasized the issue as a serious policy priority [68, 69].

CHAPTER 3

Age Verification Regulations

The question of how to protect children from harmful online content while preserving privacy and freedom of expression has become one of the most pressing regulatory challenges of the digital age. Nations worldwide are grappling with a fundamental tension: the imperative to keep minors safe online versus the need to protect the rights of adults to access lawful content and the privacy rights of all citizens. This chapter examines how different countries have approached this challenge. The regulatory responses vary dramatically across jurisdictions, shaped by distinct legal traditions, privacy frameworks, and cultural priorities. From the comprehensive statutory requirements of the United States, where 24 states have passed specific age verification mandates, to the emerging privacy-preserving approaches of Canada and the technology-agnostic directives of the European Union, no unified global standard has emerged. Instead, we see a blend of different approaches, each reflecting local values and regulatory philosophies.

DOI: 10.1201/9781003643517-3

3.1 THE UNITED STATES

The United States has developed a fragmented regulatory landscape rather than a single federal age verification system. As of recent legislative tracking, more than a dozen states have enacted laws related to age verification for online content or social media, reflecting rapid and ongoing policy development rather than a stable national framework. This decentralized approach reflects American constitutional principles regarding federalism, yet it creates substantial compliance challenges for digital services operating across state lines [70].

American state laws addressing age verification fall into three primary categories, each responding to different perceived harms to minors online. The dominant category comprises "harmful to minors" (HTM) laws, currently enacted in 19 states. These laws target material deemed obscene under the Miller test—a three-part standard requiring that content appeal to prurient interests, depict sexual conduct in a patently offensive manner, and lack serious literary, artistic, political, or scientific value. States including Texas, Utah, and Tennessee have enacted HTM legislation requiring commercial entities to verify that individuals accessing such material are at least 18 years old.

The second category addresses social media safety. Six states—Arkansas, Louisiana, Georgia, Mississippi, Texas, and Utah—have enacted laws requiring parental consent for minors to create or maintain social media accounts and mandating platforms to verify user age. These laws reflect growing concerns about addiction, mental health impacts, and exploitation of young users through algorithmic content promotion. A third, smaller category of laws, including California's Age-Appropriate Design Code Act and Maryland's Kids Code, takes a broader approach, requiring age verification for any online service likely to be accessed by children, without restricting the request to specific content categories.

Most US laws establish 18 years as the age threshold for restricted content, aligning with federal standards. However, social media laws show greater variation, with some states setting 16 as the threshold and others recognizing exceptions for emancipated or married minors. This lack of harmonization creates practical compliance difficulties: how should platforms distinguish between a 16-year-old in Ohio (where a social media law sets that threshold) and a 16-year-old in California (where the threshold is 18)?

The methods for verification permitted under these laws reflect a spectrum of approaches. Government-issued identification remains the most commonly specified method, appearing in 14 state laws. Digitized identification—digital copies of driver's licenses or state ID cards—appears in 12 state laws, reflecting emerging technological capabilities. Transactional data approaches, which verify age through financial history, purchasing patterns, or credit checks, also appear in 12 states. Notably, most states permit "any commercially reasonable method," providing flexibility but creating uncertainty about what technologies qualify as commercially reasonable.

Numerous state laws face constitutional challenges based on First Amendment grounds. Courts have raised concerns about whether age verification requirements are narrowly tailored to achieve compelling government interests in protecting children, or whether they impose excessive burdens on adults' access to lawful content. The Arkansas Social Media Safety Act was preliminarily enjoined in 2023 after courts found it unconstitutionally vague regarding which entities fell within its scope. Similarly, preliminary injunctions have been granted against laws in Indiana, Mississippi, Ohio, and Utah, with findings that the restrictions fail strict scrutiny analysis—the demanding constitutional standard applied to laws restricting protected speech.

The Texas "Harmful to Minors" law has reached the Supreme Court, which agreed to hear the case in 2024. The main question is whether states can require adults to verify their age before accessing legal sexual content, even if this may discourage free speech [71].

What emerges from the US landscape is a regulatory environment defined by disagreement about fundamental questions: What methods of verification are sufficiently privacy-protective? How much burden may be placed on adults to access lawful content? How can verification occur while minimizing identity collection? Which entities should bear responsibility for verification—platforms, content providers, payment processors, or device manufacturers?

The lack of federal coordination has generated proposals for national standards. The Kids Online Safety and Privacy Act, proposed at the federal level, would require the Secretary of Commerce to study device-level or operating system-level age verification methods. Yet even this proposal acknowledges that no universally accepted methodology currently exists [72].

3.2 THE EUROPEAN UNION

The European regulatory approach emphasizes proportionality, privacy by design, and flexibility in implementation. This approach reflects European legal traditions prioritizing fundamental rights—both children's protection and adults' and minors' rights to access information, alongside robust privacy safeguards.

Three primary legislative instruments shape the EU approach. The General Data Protection Regulation (GDPR) establishes baseline data protection requirements, including provisions addressing children's special protections—particularly around consent and data processing. The Digital Services Act (DSA), enacted in 2022 and entering enforcement in 2024–2025, establishes obligations for online platforms to address systemic risks to minors, including harms from inappropriate content, algorithmic amplification of harmful material, and manipulative design practices. The Audiovisual Media Services Directive (AVMSD) specifically addresses media content regulation, with age-related requirements for audiovisual services.

What distinguishes the EU framework is its insistence that age assurance cannot justify data maximization. Under GDPR principles and DSA accountability requirements, service providers must demonstrate that verification methods employ data minimization, collecting only essential information for age confirmation. This principle has led some jurisdictions to explore technological approaches permitting age confirmation without identity disclosure: for instance, biometric age verification systems that process images locally on a device, returning only a binary age determination without storing biometric data or transmitting identifying information to service providers.

Rather than prescribing specific technologies, the EU has commissioned the development of an "age verification blueprint" and is piloting an "EU Digital Identity" (EUDI) wallet system. These initiatives aim to create interoperable standards that would enable citizens to prove they meet age thresholds while minimizing personal data collection. The EUDI wallet approach—conceptually similar to a digital driver's license stored on a citizen's phone—would allow proof of age status without disclosing personal identity information to service providers [73].

This approach reflects a child-rights-focused philosophy: the goal is not merely to prevent harmful content access, but to accomplish this through methods that simultaneously protect privacy and data security. The framework presumes that privacy protection and child protection are complementary goals, not competing ones. A teenager who discloses minimal personal information while accessing lawful age-restricted content faces lower risks of data harvesting, profiling, and manipulation than one whose full identity must be verified with each access attempt across numerous platforms.

Additionally, several member states have implemented specific age verification requirements. France enacted the SREN Law in 2024, requiring pornographic websites to implement reliable age verification through ID verification or biometric methods. The country's broadcasting regulator, ARCOM, has established technical standards for compliance [74]. Germany has similarly updated its Youth Media Protection Act (JMStV) to align with DSA principles while maintaining age verification requirements for youth-endangering content [75].

Ireland's Online Safety Code 2024 similarly requires platforms to implement age verification systems but within a proportionality framework. Services with minimal child risk may implement less intrusive verification approaches [76].

On April 15, 2026, the European Commission announced that their new age verification app designed to protect children online is ready for deployment and will soon be available for citizens to use. The new age verification app is user-friendly and can be set up using a passport or ID card, enabling users to prove their age when accessing online services. The app is completely anonymous, works on any device, and is fully open source [77].

3.3 THE UNITED KINGDOM

The United Kingdom has emerged as a global pioneer in regulating online safety and age assurance, with its framework evolving through a long policy process that began in 2017. Early momentum came from growing concern over children's exposure to harmful online content, cyberbullying, and algorithm-driven risks on large digital platforms. In 2019, the UK government formally launched the Online Harms White Paper, which proposed a new regulatory regime requiring platforms to take responsibility for user safety, especially for children. This marked the first structured step toward what would later become the Online Safety framework [78].

In 2021, the proposal evolved into the Online Safety Bill, which significantly strengthened platform obligations, introducing statutory "duty of care" requirements and giving regulators authority to enforce compliance. Over the following years, the bill was debated and refined, with increasing emphasis on child protection, transparency, and accountability of social media companies and content providers [79].

This legislative process culminated in the Online Safety Act in 2023, which established a comprehensive legal framework for regulating online harms. A key feature of this system is mandatory age assurance for high-risk services, particularly pornography platforms. Notably, the UK framework explicitly permits privacy-preserving and anonymity-preserving verification methods, allowing users to confirm age eligibility without disclosing full identity to content providers. This reflects the principle that privacy protection and child safety can coexist [80].

The framework is enforced by the UK communications regulator, Ofcom, which is responsible for overseeing compliance, evaluating age assurance systems, and taking regulatory action where necessary. This centralized model contrasts with more fragmented approaches such as in the United States, where regulation varies by state.

In July 2025, the UK transitioned from legislation to full-scale implementation of mandatory age assurance requirements for pornographic websites. This marked a major global milestone, positioning the UK as a pioneer in operationalizing national-level, enforceable age verification.

3.4 CANADA

Canada presents a distinct approach to age verification, shaped strongly by its privacy-oriented legal tradition along with its unique local context of grassroots campaigns. The country hosts the world's largest adult content platform, which has contributed to growing public concern and intense campaigns for stronger child protection online. This has aligned Canada well with global discussions on mandatory age verification, particularly for preventing minors' access to sexually explicit content.

However, Canada's regulatory development is influenced by strong privacy protections under federal laws, particularly the Personal Information Protection and Electronic Documents Act (PIPEDA), along with provincial privacy frameworks. As a result, policymakers have emphasized that any age verification system must minimize data collection and avoid unnecessary identity disclosure.

Legislative efforts have primarily emerged in the Canadian Senate. It started with "Bill S-210: An Act to restrict young persons' online access to sexually explicit material" introduced in 2021. It requires pornographic websites to implement age verification and allows courts to order internet service providers to block non-compliant platforms. It passed the Senate unanimously in 2023 and advanced in the House of Commons, but its progress stalled following the 2025 federal election. A follow-up proposal, Bill S-209, introduced in May 2025 and approved in the Senate in April 2026, continues this legislative direction by seeking to strengthen restrictions on minors' access to online pornographic content. Overall, Canada's approach reflects a careful balancing act: strong concern for online child safety alongside a deep commitment to privacy principles, resulting in gradual and incremental movement toward formal age verification regulation [43–46].

3.5 AUSTRALIA

Australia's path to large-scale age assurance in 2025 reflects a gradual evolution from platform accountability to enforceable access controls. The foundation was laid with the Online Safety Act 2021, which established a comprehensive regulatory framework placing responsibility on digital platforms to address harmful and age-restricted content. Rather than mandating specific technologies, the Act emphasized industry-developed codes of practice, overseen by the eSafety Commissioner and the Australian Communications and Media Authority (ACMA), allowing flexibility while holding platforms accountable for outcomes.

In the years following 2021, regulatory attention increasingly focused on gaps in protecting minors, particularly the widespread use of social media by children below minimum age thresholds. Studies and regulatory findings showed that large numbers of children—especially those aged 8–12—were accessing platforms through weak self-declaration systems, highlighting the limitations of existing approaches. In response, Australia initiated policy reviews and national age assurance technology trials to evaluate the effectiveness, accuracy, and privacy implications of different verification methods, including biometric estimation, document checks, and device-based signals.

By 2025, informed by trial outcomes and growing public concern over youth online harms, Australia implemented mandatory obligations requiring platforms to take "reasonable steps" to prevent under-16 users from accessing social media services. This marked a significant transition from a primarily industry-led model to enforceable, outcome-based regulation, while still preserving flexibility in how platforms implement age assurance [81–83].

3.6 OTHER NOTABLE EXAMPLES

China: China represents one of the most stringent age verification regimes globally, relying on centralized state control and mandatory identity systems. The government requires real-name registration across digital services, supported by biometric tools such as facial recognition, particularly in gaming and social media. Minors face strict usage limits—for example, online gaming is restricted to a few hours per week—and compliance is enforced through a centralized authority with strong penalties, creating a highly controlled digital ecosystem focused on youth protection [84].

India: India's approach to age verification is fragmented and evolving, shaped by a combination of national laws and state-level regulations. While the country broadly restricts access to pornographic content and requires platforms to remove harmful material under IT Rules 2021, age verification practices vary across sectors such as gaming, e-commerce, and alcohol sales. Enforcement often relies on ISP blocking and platform responsibility rather than a unified verification system, reflecting ongoing efforts to strengthen digital child safety while managing legal complexity [85].

Singapore: Singapore follows a balanced model that combines strict regulation with strong data protection principles. Age verification is required for specific services such as online gambling and restricted content, often integrated with national identity systems like SingPass. At the same time, the country emphasizes privacy through its Personal Data Protection Act and promotes industry collaboration and public awareness campaigns, aiming to protect minors without undermining innovation or data security [86].

South Korea: South Korea is a leader in digital age verification, using national identity numbers and mobile carrier data to enforce age restrictions across gaming, social media, and adult content. Policies such as the "Cinderella Law" (nighttime gaming restrictions for minors) illustrate the country's proactive stance. Supported by strong enforcement and public awareness initiatives, South Korea maintains a comprehensive system that integrates verification across multiple digital sectors [87].

Japan: Japan adopts a structured and technology-integrated approach to age verification, often linking verification to mobile carriers and national identity systems such as "My Number." Age checks are widely applied across services including gaming, social media, dating platforms, and adult content. In April 2026, Japan's Ministry of Internal Affairs and Communications proposed requiring social media platforms to implement stricter age verification to address issues such as youth addiction and bullying. [88].

Spain: Spain's approach is closely aligned with broader European Union regulation. The country is actively exploring and piloting digital identity-based age assurance systems, including EU digital wallet initiatives, particularly for restricting access to pornographic content. In February 2026, Spain announced plans to ban social media for under-16s [89].

South Africa: South Africa's approach to online safety and age assurance is still emerging, supported by data protection laws and child online protection policies. Age verification is not yet systematically mandated, but discussions are ongoing around strengthening protections for minors in online environments [90].

Malaysia: Malaysia is implementing a stringent age verification framework under its Online Safety Act 2025. The government plans to introduce a minimum social media age of 16 in the second half of 2026. The framework may leverage eKYC processes and national digital identity infrastructure such as MyKad and MyDigital ID. The approach emphasizes platform accountability while seeking to balance child safety with data privacy considerations [91].

Indonesia: Indonesia has adopted an enforcement-driven approach to age verification under Ministerial Regulation No. 9 of 2026, requiring digital platforms to prevent users under 16 from accessing high-risk social media services. The policy mandates age verification mechanisms and account deactivation for underage users, with enforcement beginning in March 2026. Platforms must also conduct risk assessments and implement child safety measures, including controls on interactions and content exposure. Thus Indonesia became the first Asian country to ban social media for under-16s [91].

3.7 AGE VERIFICATION PROVIDERS ASSOCIATION (AVPA)

Founded in 2018, the Age Verification Providers Association (AVPA) serves as the global trade association representing age assurance providers [92]. With 30+ members as of 2025, it establishes industry standards for independent auditing, privacy-by-design principles, and interoperability frameworks. The association advocates for proportionate age checks that balance safety with privacy. AVPA members work collaboratively with regulators across jurisdictions to harmonize technical specifications and promote best practices that ensure regulatory compliance.

CHAPTER 4

Age Verification Standards

WITH AN INCREASING GLOBAL demand, multiple age verification approaches have emerged, each carrying different levels of accuracy, privacy implications, and implementation complexity. This diversity necessitates standards that align technical solutions with local regulatory requirements while maintaining global interoperability.

4.1 IEEE 2089.1: STANDARD FOR ONLINE AGE VERIFICATION

The Institute of Electrical and Electronics Engineers (IEEE) published IEEE 2089.1 in May 2024 to establish a comprehensive framework for designing, specifying, evaluating, and deploying online age verification systems. Centered on children's digital rights, this standard provides processes for digital services to verify or estimate user age with proportionate accuracy [93].

To avoid a one-size-fits-all approach, IEEE 2089.1 introduces a multi-dimensional confidence framework featuring six indicators of assurance:

DOI: 10.1201/9781003643517-4

- Accuracy: 4 levels
- Frequency of Assurance: 4 levels
- Counter-Fraud Measures: 3 levels
- Authenticity: 4 levels
- Frequency of Authenticity: 4 levels
- Birth Date Verification: 3 levels

This structure enables organizations to calibrate verification rigor proportionate to risk. The standard emphasizes privacy preservation, data security, and cross-platform interoperability while facilitating regulatory compliance. Furthermore, the IEEE Standards Association established a certification program that assesses system design against these requirements, providing reliable assurance to regulators and stakeholders.

4.2 ISO/IEC 27566-1:2025: FRAMEWORK FOR AGE ASSURANCE SYSTEMS

Published in December 2025 by the International Organization for Standardization (ISO) and the International Electrotechnical Commission (IEC), ISO/IEC 27566-1:2025 integrates age assurance within the broader domain of information security, cybersecurity, and privacy protection [94]. This 29-page standard establishes core principles for age-related eligibility decisions without prescribing specific technical implementations. A key innovation is the concept of variable assurance levels. High-stakes contexts require intense verification processes, potentially utilizing third-party services or aggregating multiple age indicators. Low-stakes contexts permit simpler, faster approaches to minimize friction and data collection. Designed to complement IEEE 2089.1, ISO/IEC 27566-1 provides globally harmonized guidance for proportional risk assessment. A forthcoming Part 2 will offer detailed technical specifications for system components, communication protocols, and stakeholder interactions.

4.3 AGE CHECK CERTIFICATION SCHEME

Approved by the UK Information Commissioner's Office (ICO) in 2021, the Age Check Certification Scheme (ACCS) is the first data protection-focused certification scheme for age assurance products. Operating as a UKAS-accredited conformity assessment body, ACCS utilizes auditors and data protection experts to test verification systems [95].

ACCS 2:2021 establishes baseline data protection criteria for organizations using verification, estimation, and inference methods. In 2026, ACCS expanded its portfolio to incorporate ISO/IEC 27566-1, creating a unified global certification scheme supported by IEEE-approved laboratory testing.

ACCS certification ensures compliance with the UK Age-Appropriate Design Code (the Children's Code). It emphasizes proportionality. Organizations must match their assurance approaches to the specific risks children face on their platforms, ensuring robust protection against significant harms while preventing excessive data collection in low-risk scenarios.

4.4 EUROPEAN UNION: AGE VERIFICATION BLUEPRINT

In October 2025, the European Commission released an enhanced second version of its age verification blueprint. This framework provides technical specifications aligned with the EU Digital Identity Wallet and open-source implementations adaptable to national contexts, directly supporting the provisions of the Digital Services Act (DSA) [96]. Its key features are:

- Onboarding: Support for passports and identity cards alongside electronic IDs (eIDs) to generate age proofs.
- API Integration: Integration with the Digital Credentials API for seamless proof presentation in modern browsers and operating systems.

- Standardized Architecture: Built on ISO/IEC 18013-5 (mobile driving licenses) and ISO/IEC 23220-2 (identity management).

It serves as a reference standard for device-based, privacy-preserving age verification, maintaining technical interoperability across member states.

4.5 CANADA: CAN/DGSI 127:2025

Canada's Digital Governance Standards Institute published "CAN/DGSI 127:2025—Age Assurance Technologies" in August 2025. This principles-based framework sets minimum requirements for technologies verifying age or estimating age ranges. Crucially, CAN/DGSI 127 mandates a Child Rights Impact Assessment (CRIA) before implementation, ensuring children's rights inform system design from inception. The standard is platform-agnostic and categorizes age verification into different methods suited for varying risk levels [97].

4.6 INTERNET SOCIETY: GUIDING PRINCIPLES FOR AGE RESTRICTIONS

Rather than providing technical specifications, the Internet Society (ISOC) published a policy brief in December 2025 establishing governance and policy principles. ISOC emphasizes that while age checks are well-intentioned, they pose significant risks to privacy, security, and the open Internet. ISOC's core mandate is that age checks must not identify or track people online. Strict implementation requirements include avoiding mandatory government ID checks, limiting data sharing to age range only, and ensuring independent oversight [98].

ISOC categorizes age checks into three types, explicitly noting their trade-offs:

- Age Verification: High accuracy, but creates high security risks and access barriers.

- Age Estimation: Moderate accuracy with moderate privacy concerns.
- Self-Declaration: Low accuracy, but preserves easy access and minimal privacy risks.

ISOC has criticized specific legislative proposals (like Canada's Bill S-210 and Texas's mandatory age laws) for weakening internet privacy, advocating instead for robust governance frameworks over mere technical compliance.

4.7 COMPARATIVE ANALYSIS OF THE MAJOR STANDARDS

Despite diverse jurisdictional priorities, current age verification standards demonstrate substantial convergence around core principles, such as:

- Privacy Preservation and Data Minimization: This is common across all frameworks. ISO/IEC 27566-1 and CAN/DGSI 127 explicitly prioritize minimal data extraction, while ISOC requires limiting data to age-range outputs only.
- Proportionality: All standards agree that verification rigor must match the risk level of the digital environment, preventing excessive data collection for low-stakes contexts.
- Technology Neutrality: Frameworks acknowledge multiple valid approaches (e.g., CAN/DGSI's seven categories) rather than mandating a single technology, allowing room for innovation.

There also remain several points of divergence:

- Prescriptiveness: IEEE 2089.1 provides highly detailed technical metrics, whereas ISO/IEC 27566-1 establishes broad principles.

- Local Priorities: The EU emphasizes state-backed digital identity infrastructure, while Canada distinctively emphasizes child rights ethics.

The proliferation of distinct standards creates substantial compliance complexity for platforms operating internationally. For example, a user verified under Canada's CAN/DGSI 127 standards may not seamlessly access age-restricted content on a platform utilizing the EU Blueprint's specific cryptographic architecture without undergoing secondary verification.

Age verification standards must remain agile to keep pace with evolving technological capabilities. Ultimately, successful age verification standardization requires ongoing collaboration among technical bodies, privacy authorities, child rights advocates, and policymakers. The goal remains clear: developing harmonized, interoperable frameworks that effectively perform age verification without compromising global digital rights.

CHAPTER 5

Deploying Age Verification

Real World Impact

5.1 AGE VERIFICATION FOR ONLINE PORNOGRAPHY IN THE UNITED KINGDOM (2025)

The United Kingdom's approach to age assurance reflects a long and iterative policy trajectory shaped by concerns over child protection, technological feasibility, and digital rights. Early regulatory attempts, most notably under the Digital Economy Act 2017, sought to introduce mandatory age checks for online pornography. However, these efforts were ultimately abandoned due to implementation challenges, including the absence of enforceable mechanisms, concerns over user privacy, and uncertainty regarding the role of third-party verification providers. Despite this initial setback, the rapid growth of online content consumption—particularly among minors—kept the issue firmly on the policy agenda. Studies and policy briefings frequently indicated that a majority of UK teenagers had

DOI: 10.1201/9781003643517-5

encountered online pornography, often unintentionally and at increasingly younger ages, highlighting the limitations of self-regulatory mechanisms.

Momentum was regained with the introduction of the Online Safety Act 2023, which reframed the regulatory approach by placing a statutory duty of care on digital platforms. Rather than targeting specific websites in isolation, the Act required platforms hosting harmful content, including pornography, to take proactive measures to prevent underage access. This marked a significant shift from earlier, more fragmented regulatory attempts toward a comprehensive, system-level governance model. Public discourse during this period increasingly emphasized the inadequacy of self-declaration mechanisms, such as simple "I am over 18" click-throughs, which were widely regarded as ineffective barriers. By 2024–2025, a convergence of political will, regulatory clarity, and technological maturity created the conditions for large-scale deployment, positioning the UK as a leading jurisdiction in operationalizing age assurance at scale [78–80].

The enforcement phase began on July 25, 2025, under the supervision of Ofcom, which was designated as the primary authority responsible for overseeing compliance with the Online Safety Act. Adult websites accessible within the UK were required to implement robust age verification or estimation systems capable of demonstrating a high level of assurance that users are over 18. This requirement fundamentally altered the operational model of online pornography platforms. A range of technical solutions was used during implementation, including verification through government-issued identification, credit card authentication, and AI-driven facial age estimation systems that analyze a user's selfie to estimate age. The involvement of specialized third-party providers became central to the ecosystem, enabling platforms to outsource compliance while maintaining a degree of separation from user data.

Ofcom's enforcement was notably strong. The regulator was empowered to impose substantial financial penalties—up to £18 million or 10% of global annual turnover—as well as to require internet service providers to block access to non-compliant websites. Early enforcement actions included formal investigations into dozens of high-traffic pornographic platforms and the issuance of compliance deadlines backed by the threat of escalating sanctions. Importantly, the scope of enforcement extended beyond traditional adult websites to include platforms that host or facilitate user-generated explicit content, thereby broadening the regulatory perimeter. This expansive interpretation signaled a shift toward ecosystem-wide accountability, rather than a narrow focus on explicitly branded pornographic services.

The initial impact of the UK's age verification regime has been both significant and multifaceted, revealing a complex interplay between regulatory effectiveness, user behavior, and societal values. Immediately following deployment, virtual private network (VPN) applications surged in popularity, with several VPN services ranking among the most downloaded apps on Apple's UK App Store, indicating widespread attempts to bypass age verification mechanisms. At the same time, measurable behavioral shifts were observed. Major pornographic platforms experienced substantial declines in UK traffic—reports suggest reductions of up to 40–50% in some cases—indicating that the introduction of verification friction significantly altered access patterns. From a policy perspective, this reduction is often interpreted as an early indicator of success in limiting casual and underage exposure to explicit content [99–101].

Public opinion data further reinforces this interpretation. Surveys conducted eight months after implementation show that approximately 75% of UK adults support online age verification laws, demonstrating sustained societal backing for the policy [102]. Similarly, other studies report that a clear majority of the public believes such measures are necessary to protect children online, even if they introduce some level of inconvenience. This level of public support has provided regulators with legitimacy and resilience against any pushback, strengthening the long-term viability of this regulatory framework.

At the same time, privacy concerns remain at the forefront, particularly regarding the collection, processing, and potential misuse of sensitive personal data. Advocacy groups and digital rights organizations have highlighted risks associated with biometric verification and identity-linked access, warning of potential data breaches. There are also concerns about market impacts. Compliance costs, both technical and legal, are significantly higher for smaller operators. This is potentially leading to market consolidation where larger platforms dominate due to their greater capacity to absorb regulatory burdens.

In October 2025, just three months after the implementation of mandatory age checks, Pornhub said the number of UK visitors to its website was down 77% compared with July [103]. In February 2026, it announced it would restrict access in the UK, allowing only existing, age verified users to continue using the site. The company argues the age verification law has been ineffective, claiming it reduces traffic on regulated platforms while pushing users, especially minors, toward less regulated and potentially riskier websites [104].

Overall, the UK's 2025 rollout represents one of the most comprehensive real-world implementations of age verification for adult content to date. It demonstrates that large-scale enforcement is technically and institutionally feasible. As such, it serves as a model for other jurisdictions considering similar interventions.

5.2 AGE VERIFICATION FOR SOCIAL MEDIA IN AUSTRALIA (2025)

The Australian approach to age assurance for social media platforms represents another landmark regulatory intervention in online child safety governance. On December 10,

2025, Australia implemented the world's first social media age restrictions, requiring major platforms to prevent users under the age of 16 from creating or maintaining accounts. According to guidance issued by the eSafety Commissioner of Australia, these restrictions apply broadly to major services including Facebook, Instagram, TikTok, Snapchat, YouTube, X (formerly Twitter), Reddit, Twitch, and other social media platforms.

The policy emerged in response to long-standing evidence that children were widely exposed to social media platforms despite nominal minimum age requirements. Prior regulatory assessments found that a substantial proportion of children aged 8–12 were already active users of social media, with around 80% of children in this age group using at least one platform, and an estimated 1.3 million children potentially accessing services in violation of platform age policies. Furthermore, only 36% of children aged 8–12 who used social media had their own account, and a significant share of those accounts were created with parental assistance or through simple self-declaration mechanisms, highlighting weaknesses.

To address these gaps, the 2025 framework introduced mandatory obligations that require platforms to implement age verification through suitable mechanisms like document-based, behavioral, or facial image-based age checks. The regulatory structure is embedded within broader online safety governance frameworks, which extend protections against exposure to harmful and age-inappropriate content across multiple digital service categories [81, 82].

Its implementation has been supported by extensive regulatory guidance and technical evaluation initiatives. A large-scale independent trial was conducted in Australia to evaluate whether modern age assurance technologies are capable of operating in real-world conditions while maintaining privacy, security, and usability. The findings of this trial recommended a technologically mature and fast-evolving ecosystem, where multiple approaches coexist, each suited to different contexts rather than a single universal solution [83].

At the core of the study is the recognition that "age assurance" is not a single technology but a collection of methods, broadly categorized into age verification, age estimation, age inference, and hybrid models such as successive validation. These are complemented by parental control and consent systems, all operating within a broader technical infrastructure or "stack" that integrates across devices, platforms, and services. Across the trial, 48 technology providers participated, offering diverse implementation options.

Age verification represents the most direct and high-assurance approach. It works by linking an individual to a verified date of birth obtained from authoritative sources such as identity documents or official records. Vendors in this category typically combine document scanning, database checks, and biometric matching to ensure that the person presenting the credential is its legitimate owner. The results indicate that such systems are already highly reliable. In large-scale testing involving nearly twelve thousand interactions, leading solutions achieved accuracy levels exceeding 97 percent, with relatively low false acceptance and rejection rates. Many vendors also implemented privacy-preserving techniques, such as returning only a binary outcome (e.g., "over 18") rather than revealing full identity data. Increasingly, these systems are integrating with digital wallets, allowing users to reuse verified credentials without repeated identity checks.

Alongside verification, age estimation technologies offer a different approach. Instead of relying on official records, these systems use artificial intelligence models—often trained on facial or behavioral data—to predict a user's likely age range. Vendors in this space emphasize low friction and anonymity, making their solutions particularly attractive in contexts where collecting identity documents would be intrusive or impractical. The trial found that these systems are technically deployable across standard consumer devices and are improving steadily in accuracy. However, their probabilistic nature introduces limitations, especially in high-risk scenarios where precise age determination is required. Performance also varies under less controlled conditions, such as poor lighting or camera quality, highlighting areas where further refinement is needed.

A third category, age inference, operates more indirectly by analyzing patterns in user behavior, metadata, or contextual signals to estimate age. While not as prominent in high-assurance use cases, these systems demonstrate the growing role of data analytics in shaping digital identity. Their effectiveness depends heavily on data availability and raises more complex ethical questions around profiling and transparency.

Many vendors are moving toward layered or hybrid approaches, combining multiple techniques in what the report describes as "successive validation." In these systems, a low-friction method such as age estimation may be used initially, with more robust verification triggered only when risk thresholds are exceeded. This adaptive model allows service providers to balance usability with security, applying stricter checks only when necessary.

Parental control technologies form another important component of the ecosystem. These systems shift responsibility toward guardians, either by enabling ongoing control over a child's digital environment or by requiring explicit approval at key access points. The trial found that while these tools can be effective, they introduce tensions around children's autonomy and evolving digital rights. Such systems may not adapt well as children mature, as they encourage more dynamic interaction but rely on active parental engagement.

Across all these categories, the vendor landscape appears highly dynamic. The trial highlights a vibrant and competitive industry, characterized by continuous innovation and increasing alignment with international standards. Many providers demonstrated advanced capabilities and readiness for deployment, indicating that they are already functioning in operational environments. At the same time, newer approaches—such as cryptographic verification and privacy-preserving data exchanges—are emerging from earlier stages of development, suggesting significant future evolution.

From a performance perspective, one of the most notable findings is the consistency across demographic groups. Despite concerns about bias in AI-driven systems, the technologies tested generally produced stable results across different populations, including indigenous communities. While some gaps remain—particularly due to underrepresentation in training data—the overall variation stayed within acceptable limits. This suggests that fairness, while not fully resolved, is being actively addressed by vendors.

Privacy and data security emerged as central design priorities across the sector. Most systems follow a "privacy-by-design" approach, minimizing data collection and avoiding long-term storage of sensitive information. Techniques such as tokenization, session-based authentication, and selective disclosure are becoming standard practice. However, the trial also identified a concerning trend among some providers toward excessive data retention, often justified by anticipated regulatory requirements. This creates unnecessary risk and underscores the need for clearer policy guidance.

Cybersecurity performance was generally strong. Vendors demonstrated resilience against common threats, including spoofing attacks, forged documents, and increasingly sophisticated AI-generated manipulations. Biometric systems frequently incorporated liveness detection to ensure that real users, rather than synthetic inputs, were being evaluated. Nonetheless, the report emphasizes that the threat landscape is constantly evolving, and no system can be considered entirely secure without continuous monitoring and updates.

Despite these positive findings, several practical challenges remain. Usability continues to be a key barrier, particularly for less technically literate users. Integration across platforms and interoperability between systems also require further development. In some cases, access to authoritative data—such as real-time validation of lost or stolen identity documents—is limited. Additionally, digital exclusion in remote or underserved communities poses a structural challenge that cannot be solved by technology alone.

Ultimately, the trial showed that age verification technologies are not only feasible but already operational at scale, with no fundamental technical barriers preventing their deployment. However, their effectiveness depends heavily on context, implementation choices, and governance frameworks. No single method can address all use cases. Instead, a flexible combination of approaches is required.

The key takeaway from this trial was that age assurance is no longer a theoretical concept but a practical, deployable reality. A diverse ecosystem of technologies—ranging from high-assurance identity verification to low-friction AI estimation—is already capable of supporting age-based controls across digital environments. Most vendors demonstrated strong performance, growing maturity, and a clear commitment to privacy and security.

However, the real challenge is no longer technological but systemic. Effective deployment will depend on thoughtful integration, regulatory clarity, and careful balancing of competing priorities: privacy versus accountability, security versus usability, and protection versus autonomy. In this sense, the future of age verification will be shaped less by breakthroughs in technology and more by how societies choose to govern and apply the tools that already exist.

Despite the positive indications from the trial, early evidence suggests that enforcement effectiveness remains uneven after the deployment. Recent post-implementation studies indicated that more than 60% of underage users in Australia still retain access to social media platforms, either through bypass techniques, account retention, or weak enforcement mechanisms. It suggested that over 50% of previously identified underage users on major platforms such as TikTok, YouTube, and Instagram continue to access services even after the enforcement. These findings highlight persistent challenges in operationalizing age verification at this scale, particularly in environments where users can easily misrepresent age or migrate between platforms.

61% of parents of children aged 16 and under saw between two and four positive behavioral changes following the ban, including more in-person social interactions, improved parent–child relationships, and children being more present and engaged during interactions. However, two in five parents observed between two and four negative impacts, including increased digital inequality, a shift to alternative or less regulated platforms, and a reduction in social connection.

Additional reporting suggests that while social media platforms initially claimed the removal or restriction of approximately 4.7 million underage accounts, yet this figure has not translated into equivalent reductions in actual user access, reinforcing concerns about the difference between account enforcement and real-world behavioral outcomes. Early qualitative evidence from UNICEF Australia suggests that young people are adapting to the restrictions through alternative navigation strategies, including alternative accounts, shared devices, or identity misrepresentation strategies [105–107].

Overall, Australia's 2025 age assurance framework illustrates both the ambition and complexity of embedding age-based access control into social media infrastructure. While the policy has achieved significant regulatory alignment and industry compliance momentum, early evidence indicates that technical bypass methods and behavioral adaptation among users continue to limit its effectiveness. As such, the Australian case contributes important insight into the global debate on age verification, demonstrating that while regulatory frameworks can reshape platform obligations, achieving consistent real-world exclusion of underage users in social media remains a persistent technical and socio-behavioral challenge.

5.3 COMPARATIVE PERSPECTIVES: UNITED KINGDOM VS. AUSTRALIA

The United Kingdom and Australia represent two of the most prominent national approaches to age verification till the start of 2026, each reflecting different regulatory priorities while sharing a common goal of strengthening child online safety. Although both jurisdictions deploy age verification mechanisms, they differ in scope, implementation context, and regulatory framing.

In the United Kingdom, age assurance is primarily applied to adult content, particularly pornographic websites. The focus is therefore on content-specific restriction, where age checks act as a gatekeeping mechanism at the point of entry to high-risk material. The regulatory model is relatively centralized, supported by strong enforcement powers, including financial penalties and the ability to restrict access to non-compliant sites.

In Australia, the 2025 framework takes a broader approach by focusing on social media access for users under 16, rather than specific content types. Major platforms are required to take "reasonable steps" to prevent underage account creation and continued use. This includes the integration of age assurance tools such as identity checks, behavioral signals, and AI-based estimation techniques. Compared to the UK, Australia's model is more focused on platform participation itself, embedding age assurance within the account creation and login process across multiple social media services.

The early outcomes in both jurisdictions show different patterns of impact. In the UK, initial reports suggest a noticeable reduction in traffic to pornographic websites following the introduction of verification requirements. In Australia, early evidence suggests that while platforms have implemented a range of compliance measures, a proportion of underage users continue to access social media services, reflecting the ongoing challenge of enforcing age restrictions in highly networked and user-driven environments.

Public response in both countries has been generally supportive of these regulations. In the UK, public surveys indicate sustained support for age verification measures applied to adult content. In Australia, public discussion has similarly recognized the importance of protecting children online, while also highlighting considerations around usability and privacy.

From a technological perspective, both countries rely on similar categories of solutions, including document verification, facial image-based verification, and other available tools.

Overall, the UK and Australian cases illustrate two complementary applications of age verification. Together, they reflect a broader international trend toward incorporating age verification into digital governance frameworks, with each jurisdiction adapting implementation strategies to its specific policy objectives and platform ecosystems.

CHAPTER 6

Age Verification Mechanisms and Techniques

AGE VERIFICATION METHODS CAN be categorized into different categories [92, 108].

6.1 DOCUMENT-BASED VERIFICATION

Document-based verification is the most widely used method for age verification, both online and in person. It relies on official government-issued IDs—such as passports, driver's licenses, or health cards—which clearly display a person's date of birth. Because these documents are broadly recognized and trusted, they provide a strong and reliable way to confirm age.

How it works: Users upload or scan their ID using a device or application. Technologies like optical character recognition (OCR) quickly extract key details, such as the date of birth. For added security, modern smartphones can use near-field communication (NFC) to read the ID's embedded chip and confirm that the document is genuine and has not been tampered with.

DOI: 10.1201/9781003643517-6

Advantages: This method offers high accuracy and strong assurance, as it is based on official, government-verified information. It is widely accepted across countries and sectors, making it the most familiar and trusted approach for both users and service providers.

Limitations: Access to government IDs is not universal. In many parts of the global south, people may lack IDs due to cost, administrative barriers, or remote locations. Even in developed regions, some marginalized groups, such as First Nations communities, face similar challenges, leading to exclusion. Privacy is another major concern. Many users are uncomfortable uploading sensitive identity documents online due to fears of data breaches, misuse, or long-term storage of personal information. As a result, this method can create both access and trust barriers despite its high reliability.

6.2 FINANCIAL VERIFICATION

Financial verification is an increasingly popular option for age assurance. It uses the fact that banks and credit card companies already verify a person's age when they open an account. Because of this, having a valid bank account or credit card can act as a strong signal that someone is an adult.

How it works: Platforms connect securely to banking systems (often through open banking or trusted third-party services) to confirm that a user has an active financial account. They may check general signals—like whether the account shows typical adult activity—without accessing sensitive details such as exact transactions or balances. The process is usually fast.

Advantages: This method is convenient and widely available, as many people have bank accounts or payment cards. It is more privacy-friendly than document checks because users do not need to upload personal IDs. Data stays with the bank, which is already regulated and secure. It is also cost-effective and easy for businesses to scale.

Limitations: Some minors may still have access to prepaid cards or shared family accounts, which can reduce the effectiveness of this method. Availability also depends on region, as banking services are not equally accessible everywhere in the world. Millions of people without bank accounts, especially in underserved communities and in underdeveloped countries, may be excluded. Users must also give consent to share certain banking information, which some may be hesitant to do.

6.3 TOKEN-BASED VERIFICATION

Token-based assertion is a scalable and user-friendly approach where a trusted identity provider verifies a user's age once and then issues a reusable digital credential (or token). Instead of repeating the same checks across multiple platforms, users can simply present this token as proof of age.

How it works: Users first verify their age with a trusted provider, typically through a one-time process such as document verification or biometric estimation. Once verified, a secure digital credential is created and stored on the user's device (often in a digital identity app or wallet). When accessing an age-restricted service, the user shares only the required proof (e.g., "over 18" or an age range) rather than full identity details. To ensure the rightful owner is using the credential, the system may require authentication through a PIN, password, or biometrics like fingerprint or facial recognition. The platform then validates the token without needing to re-check original documents.

Advantages: This method greatly improves user experience by removing the need for repeated verification across different services. It enhances privacy by allowing users to share minimal information (such as age status instead of full identity). It is also efficient for businesses, as they can rely on trusted providers rather than building their own verification systems. Over time, it can create a more standardized and interoperable ecosystem for age assurance.

Limitations: The model depends heavily on trust in the identity provider. If the provider is compromised or not widely accepted, the system's reliability can be affected. Adoption is still growing, so not all platforms support reusable tokens yet. There are also usability considerations. Users must install and manage a digital identity app, which may create barriers for less tech-savvy individuals. Additionally, if a device is lost or compromised, misuse is not unlikely.

6.4 ONLINE PROFILE-BASED VERIFICATION

This method estimates a user's age by analyzing their digital footprint—particularly how their email address and online profiles have been used across different services. Instead of asking for documents, it uses data patterns to predict whether someone is likely above or below a certain age threshold.

How it works: When a user signs up, the system checks the history linked to their email address and online presence. This may include activities across platforms and profiles, particularly behavioral indicators such as interests, social connections, or education-related information. To confirm that the user actually owns the email, a verification code is usually sent to their inbox. Once verified, AI models analyze available data to estimate an age range. The result is a probabilistic assessment rather than a definitive proof.

Advantages: This approach is seamless and requires minimal effort from the user—no document uploads or selfies. It can work quickly in the background and is scalable across large platforms. It also avoids collecting personal documents and images, which can reduce privacy risks.

Limitations: Accuracy depends heavily on the availability and quality of data. For new users or those with limited online presence, there may not be enough information to make a reliable estimate. Results are probabilistic, not certain, which can lead to errors. There are also privacy concerns, as users may not fully understand how their online behavior and personal data are being analyzed. Additionally, access to such data may be restricted by regulations or platform policies, limiting its effectiveness.

6.5 BIOMETRIC VERIFICATION

Biometric methods represent one of the most innovative developments and growing in the field. These systems use artificial intelligence to analyze physical features to estimate or verify a user's age range without requiring identity documents.

6.5.1 Facial Image

Facial image is one of the most widely used biometric approaches for age assurance. It uses artificial intelligence to analyze facial features from a selfie or short video and estimate a user's age range.

How it works: The user is asked to take a selfie or short video using their device camera. The system first performs face detection and quality checks (e.g., ensuring proper lighting and that the face is real, not a photo or mask). AI models then analyze facial characteristics such as skin texture, facial structure, and key landmarks—to estimate age. The output is typically a predicted age or an age range, along with a confidence score. Platforms then apply a threshold (e.g., "likely over 18") to decide whether access should be granted.

Advantages: The main strength of this method is its speed and ease of use. Users can complete the process in seconds using a standard smartphone camera, with no need for documents or prior setup. It is highly scalable and supports anonymous verification without linking to identity. Recent evaluations by the National Institute of Standards and Technology (NIST) show that the technology has improved significantly over time. Average error rates (mean absolute error) have decreased from around 4.3 years in earlier systems to about 3.1 years in more recent models, with some achieving 2–3 years of error under controlled conditions [109].

Limitations: Despite these improvements, the method remains probabilistic rather than exact. Findings from the NIST also show that results can vary by several years for the same individual depending on image quality, lighting, facial expression, or accessories like glasses. Accuracy is also not uniform across populations. Performance can vary by demographic factors, with some groups experiencing higher error rates than others. In real-world conditions such as low-resolution images or non-frontal poses, accuracy can drop further. There is also a trade-off in decision thresholds. Reducing false acceptance of underage users may increase rejection of legitimate adults, impacting user experience.

6.5.2 Voice

Voice-based age estimation analyzes speech patterns to predict a user's age. It relies on acoustic features such as pitch, tone, and speech dynamics, which tend to change over time [110].

How it works: The user is asked to speak a short phrase or engage in a brief voice interaction. The system records the audio and extracts acoustic features such as pitch, frequency patterns, speech rate, and vocal tract characteristics. Machine learning models then analyze these features to estimate the user's age or age range. The output is typically a probabilistic prediction (e.g., likely over or under a certain age), sometimes with a confidence score.

Advantages: It offers a hands-free and camera-free alternative, making it useful in accessibility scenarios or low-bandwidth environments. It can be integrated into voice assistants or call-based systems, enabling seamless and passive verification.

Limitations: Accuracy can be affected by background noise, recording quality, language differences, and intentional voice modification. It is also probabilistic and less mature compared to facial estimation. Performance may vary significantly across accents, age groups, and datasets, and requires sufficient voice samples to work reliably.

6.5.3 Hand Gesture

This method estimates age by analyzing the physical characteristics of the hand, such as size, shape, skin texture, or movement patterns. Users typically provide an image of their hand gesture using a smartphone camera with the relevant App [111].

How it works: The user captures an image or performs a gesture using their device camera. The system detects the hand and extracts features such as finger length ratios, skin texture, wrinkles, and overall hand shape. AI models analyze these features to estimate age or classify the user into an age group. In some cases, dynamic gestures (e.g., hand movement) may also be analyzed to improve accuracy.

Advantages: It is simple and quick to perform, requiring only a camera and minimal user effort. It can also be useful in contexts where face-based methods are restricted or discouraged.

Limitations: Accuracy is generally lower compared to facial analysis, as hand features are less strongly linked to age. Variations in camera angle, lighting, and hand positioning can affect results.

6.5.4 Electrocardiogram

This emerging method estimates age using heart signal data collected from wearable devices such as smartwatches. It analyzes patterns in electrocardiogram (ECG) signals, which can change with age due to physiological factors.

How it works: The user's ECG signal is collected through a wearable device. The system processes the signal to extract features like heart rate variability, waveform shape, and timing intervals. AI models analyze these patterns to estimate biological age or predict an age range. The result is typically a probabilistic estimate based on physiological indicators.

TABLE 6.1 Comparing different methods of age verification

Method	Accuracy	Privacy	Scalability
Document based	High	Medium	High
Financial	Medium	Medium	High
Token based	High	High	Medium
Online profile based	Low	Medium	Medium
Facial image	Medium	Medium	High
Voice	Medium	Medium	Medium
Hand	Medium	High	Medium
ECG	Low	High	Low

Advantages: It offers a novel and potentially more robust method for age verification, less influenced by external conditions like lighting or appearance. It also avoids the need for selfies or ID documents. It offers a secure, anonymous method of age verification, as ECG signals are real-time signs of liveliness. With the growing adoption of wearable devices, this scheme can be available for wider adoption.

Limitations: This approach requires specialized hardware (e.g., ECG-enabled wearables), which limits accessibility. It is still in the early stages of research and deployment compared to other methods, and the accuracy is still to be proven. Data collection and interpretation can be complex, and there are additional privacy concerns related to sensitive health data [112].

Table 6.1 provides a comparison between different methods of age verification.

6.6 WHERE SHOULD AGE VERIFICATION OCCUR?

As age verification becomes a defining requirement of digital regulation, a central question shapes both policy and technical discourse—who should act as the gatekeeper of age—apps, platforms, browsers, or devices alongside operating systems? This question has sparked increasing tension across the technology ecosystem. The result, till now, is a layered but contested model, with multiple points of implementation.

6.6.1 Device and Operating System

Age is verified once at the user's device level and securely reused across the ecosystem.

How it works: In this model, operating systems such as Apple's iOS and Google's Android perform a one-time age verification during device setup, account creation, or app store interaction. Once verified, the system generates a secure age token stored locally on the device, which apps and websites can query via APIs (application point interface) to determine eligibility.

Advantages: This approach significantly reduces friction by eliminating repeated verification across services and enhances privacy by sharing only minimal information, such as whether a user is above a certain age threshold. It limits the exposure of sensitive personal data and enables a more standardized, ecosystem-wide framework for compliance.

Limitations: The model concentrates power in the hands of operating system providers, creating dependencies for developers and also limiting enforcement. Interoperability across platforms remains limited, and users must trust device manufacturers with sensitive verification processes.

6.6.2 App Store

App stores act as centralized checkpoints that enforce age requirements before apps are accessed.

How it works: Platforms such as the Apple App Store and Google Play verify user age at the point of app download or installation. Users may be prompted to confirm their age, and for minors, accounts are often linked to parental control systems that require consent for downloads and in-app activities.

Advantages: This model prevents access to age-restricted content before the app is installed, making enforcement more proactive. It also simplifies regulatory oversight by allowing governments to work with a smaller number of enforcement partners and integrates seamlessly with parental control ecosystems.

Limitations: App store enforcement does not extend to web-based content accessed through browsers, leaving significant gaps in coverage. It can also be bypassed through alternative app distribution methods. Developers must comply with platform policies, reducing flexibility and autonomy.

6.6.3 Platform

This is a traditional and widely used model, where individual platforms and web services remain responsible for verifying users' age directly within their own arena.

How it works: Platforms and web services implement age verification systems for designated content or services. This model remains widely used across social media, gaming, and adult content platforms.

Advantages: Platform-level verification operates independently of operating systems and app stores, making it a universally accepted option. It offers flexibility, allowing services to tailor their approach based on risk and context.

Limitations: This approach often results in repeated verification across services, increasing user friction and data exposure. Privacy risks are higher because sensitive information may be shared with multiple platforms.

6.6.4 Browser

Browsers can enable seamless, cross-site age verification.

How it works: Modern browsers can recognize and transmit age credentials generated by operating systems or trusted identity providers. Through extensions or plug-ins, browsers allow websites to verify age using stored tokens.

Advantages: Browser-level solutions offer interoperability across websites and platforms, making them highly scalable. They enhance privacy through cryptographic techniques and give users more direct control over their verification credentials.

Disadvantages: These solutions are still in early stages of deployment and lack widespread standardization. They depend heavily on user awareness and trust, which may slow adoption.

In recent years, device manufacturers such as Google and Apple have advocated for maintaining age verification at the platform layer, emphasizing efficiency and reduced user friction. Meanwhile, platforms such as Meta and Aylo are increasingly supporting age verification solutions anchored at the device/OS and app store level, arguing that upstream verification distributes responsibility more consistently across the ecosystem and minimizes duplicative checks at the content layer. Both sides continue to frame their positions around concerns related to privacy risks, fairness in enforcement, and overall user convenience [113, 114].

CHAPTER 7

Age Verification Using Electrocardiogram from Smartwatches

The electrocardiogram (ECG) is a widely used diagnostic tool in cardiology. It records the heart's electrical activity during the cardiac cycle through potential differences measured via electrodes placed in different parts of the human body. With increasing age, several ECG parameters, such as heart rate and the amplitude and duration of waveform components, undergo measurable changes. A range of clinical studies have documented age-related variations in ECG characteristics, motivating research into ECG-based age estimation [115–117].

To date, research on the relationship between ECG and age has largely focused on two main areas: clinical investigations of how ECG features vary with age and the prediction of age from ECG signals using deep learning techniques [118–123].

DOI: 10.1201/9781003643517-7

However, several gaps remain in the existing literature. While deep learning has been widely applied, there has been limited exploration of which specific ECG features are most indicative of age. In addition, prior studies have predominantly focused on predicting exact age, with little emphasis on age verification aligned with regulatory or industry-defined age groups. Furthermore, most research has relied on clinical 12-lead ECG data collected in hospital environments, which is not easily scalable or practical for everyday use. Meanwhile, the recent availability of single-lead ECGs in wearable devices has significantly improved accessibility, enabling more practical and continuous real-world applications of this technology.

7.1 DATASET

Using a FITBIT Sense smartwatch, we collected an ECG dataset comprising 220 individuals (Figure 7.1) [124]. The data collection, which occurred from June 2023 to April 2025, was conducted with ethical approval from Concordia University, along with authorization from the English Montreal School Board in Montreal for data collection from minors. Each record in the dataset includes 2,800 samples from a 30-second ECG recording collected at 250 Hz. Additionally, we documented each participant's gender and cardiac health history. The dataset included individuals aged between 3 and 78 years, with a maximum falling within the 30 to 40-year age range. Figure 7.2 shows the age distribution in our dataset. Of the 220 records, 133 were male and 87 were female. All participants, as they mentioned, were healthy with no significant history of cardiac abnormalities. Informed consent was obtained from every participant, in accordance with the ethical approval granted by Concordia University.Figure 7.3 shows the basic waveform of an ECG signal.

7.2 METHODS

The research methodology consisted of the following steps:

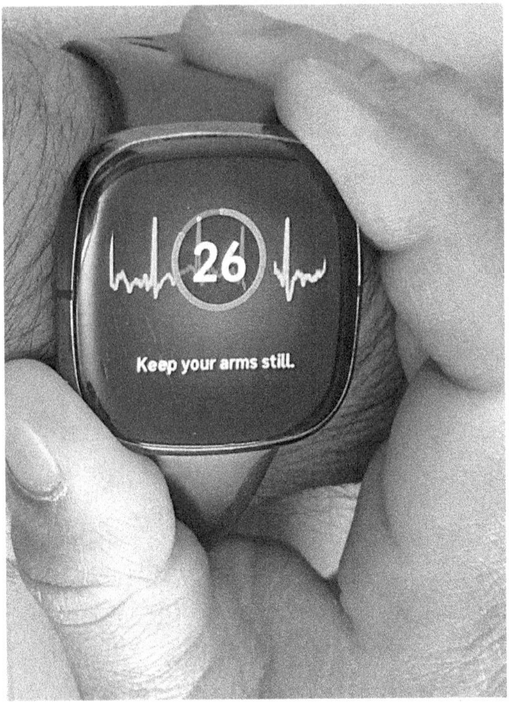

FIGURE 7.1 Capturing ECG using a smartwatch

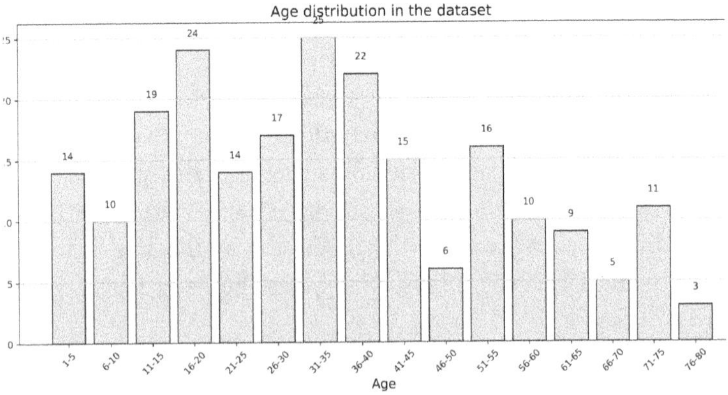

FIGURE 7.2 Histogram of age distribution in our dataset

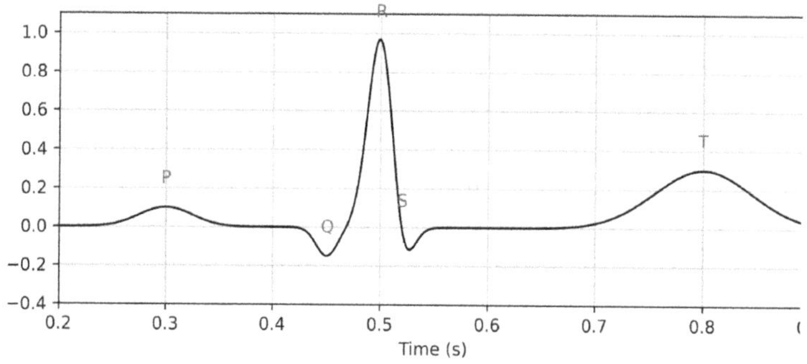

FIGURE 7.3 ECG basic waveform

i. De-noising: The major sources of noise in ECG signals include baseline wander, power line interference, and motion artifacts. To address this, we applied a 4th-order Butterworth bandpass filter on the raw ECG data for de-noising. The frequency range was adjusted based on experimental requirements, with the optimal filtering found to be in the range of 1–40 Hz.

ii. Heart Rate Variability (HRV) Analysis: We plotted HRV STD (HRV Standard Deviation, also known as SDNN) and HRV RMSSD (HRV root mean square of successive differences)—for the entire dataset, against age to better understand how heart rate variability (HRV) changes as people grow older. These two metrics are widely used. HRV STD reflects overall variability in heart rate while HRV RMSSD specifically measures short-term, beat-to-beat variability.

iii. Feature extraction: Previous studies have performed age estimation using only the core ECG signal obtained in hospital settings. In our study, we analyzed the actual ECG alongside different extracted features. To improve the interpretability of our algorithm, we used various features:

   a. Discrete Wavelet Transform (DWT): Discrete Wavelet Transform (DWT) previously yielded promising results in age estimation from ECG in our earlier research

[124–125]. DWT decomposes a signal into different levels of approximation (low-frequency components) and detail (high-frequency components) by passing it through a series of filters. The output is a set of coefficients representing the signal's detail and approximation at each level of decomposition. DWT has long been a versatile tool in ECG analysis, widely applied for tasks such as de-noising and arrhythmia detection. In our scheme, we employed ten different mother wavelets from the Daubechies family (db1 to db10) and one from the Symlet family (sym4). All the approximation and detailed coefficients were organized into a matrix, where each row represents the coefficients, providing a comprehensive representation of the signal's frequency content at multiple resolutions. This approach was made considering the factors below:

- Signal morphology matching: Each wavelet family has distinct shapes that may better match certain ECG waveform features. The range from db1 to db10 offers different levels of smoothness, allowing for the capture of both sharp transitions and smoother components in ECG signals.
- Robustness: A diverse set of features extracted using different wavelets can make the algorithm more robust to individual variations and noise. Each wavelet may highlight different aspects of the ECG signal.
- Frequency localization: Different wavelets provide varying degrees of frequency localization, which is crucial for analyzing the spectral content of ECG signals across different scales. This is more evident as heartbeat and corresponding frequencies of ECG vary with age [115–117].

b. Power Spectral Density: In ECG analysis, PSD is commonly used to study the frequency content of heart rate variability (HRV) signals, which reflect the autonomic nervous system's activity. For age analysis, PSD is particularly useful because it can reveal age-related changes in cardiovascular physiology. Different frequency bands in the PSD (e.g., low-frequency and high-frequency components) correspond to specific biological processes, such as parasympathetic and sympathetic nervous system regulation. Aging tends to alter the balance between these components, making PSD a valuable tool for extracting features that correlate with age.

iv. Deep learning: We used the following schemes:
   a. LSTM (Long Short-Term Memory): LSTMs are a type of recurrent neural network (RNN) designed to capture long-term dependencies in sequential data. They are highly effective for ECG because they can model temporal patterns and subtle variations in heart rhythms.
   b. Inception1D: Inception1D is tailored for time-series feature extraction, using parallel convolutional layers with different kernel sizes to capture patterns at multiple temporal resolutions. It can detect both short-term and long-term features in heartbeats.
   c. Feedforward Neural Network: We used a fully connected feedforward neural network designed for a regression task. It begins with an input layer that accepts features shaped according to the number of input variables in the dataset. The first hidden layer consists of 256 neurons with a ReLU activation function, followed by a dropout layer with a rate of 0.1 to reduce overfitting. The second hidden layer has 128 neurons, also using ReLU activation, and is followed by another dropout layer with the same rate. Finally, the output layer is a single neuron without an activation function, making it suitable for predicting a continuous target variable. This architecture provides a balance between learning capacity and regularization.

d. Transformer Network: We used a transformer network comprising stacked layers of multi-head self-attention mechanisms for contextual feature extraction across the full input sequence. Each sublayer is coupled with residual skip connections and layer normalization to promote stable gradient propagation and accelerate convergence. This architectural design facilitates efficient modeling of both local and long-range dependencies without recurrence or convolution. To derive a fixed-length representation compatible with downstream classification, we employed global average pooling over token embeddings, yielding a compact yet semantically enriched vector summarizing the sequence information [126].

In all the scenarios, 60% of the data was used for training, 20% was used for validation, and 20% was used for testing.

v. Performance metrics: In line with the guidelines established, we used the matrices below to evaluate performance for age estimation [127].

Mean Absolute Error (MAE):

$$\text{MAE} = \frac{1}{n}\sum_{i=1}^{n}\left|p_i - a_i\right| \tag{7.1}$$

Standard Deviation of Absolute Error (SDAE):

$$\text{SDAE} = \sqrt{\frac{1}{n-1}\sum_{i=1}^{n}\left(AE_i - MAE\right)^2} \tag{7.2}$$

Pearson's correlation coefficient (r):

$$r = \frac{n\sum_{i=1}^{n}p_i a_i - \left(\sum_{i=1}^{n}p_i\right)\left(\sum_{i=1}^{n}a_i\right)}{\sqrt{\left[n\sum_{i=1}^{n}p_i^2 - \left(\sum_{i=1}^{n}p_i\right)^2\right]\left[n\sum_{i=1}^{n}a_i^2 - \left(\sum_{i=1}^{n}a_i\right)^2\right]}} \tag{7.3}$$

where, n = Number of samples

p_i = Predicted age

a_i = Actual age

$AE_i = |p_i - a_i|$ = Absolute error for the *i-th* sample

Confidence Interval: We used the below formula for estimating the 95% confidence interval around the thresholds.

$$Confidence\ Interval, CI = \left(p - Z\sqrt{\frac{p(1-p)}{n}}, p + Z\sqrt{\frac{p(1-p)}{n}} \right) \quad (7.4)$$

where, n = Number of samples

p = Classification accuracy

$Z = 1.96$ (the Z-score corresponding to a 95% confidence level)

For age verification, we used the metrics described in Tables 7.1 and 7.2 for performance comparison.

TABLE 7.1 Performance metrics for age verification

Abbreviation	Full form	Formula
TPR	True Positive Rate (Sensitivity)	TP/(TP+FN)
TNR	True Negative Rate (Specificity)	TN/(FP+TN)
FPR	False Positive Rate (Fall-out)	FP/(FP+TN)
FNR	False Negative Rate (Miss rate)	FN/(FP+TN)
PPV	Positive Predictive Value	TP/(TP+FP)
NPV	Negative Predictive Value	TN/(TN+FN)
F1-score		(2*PPV*TPR)/(TPR+PPV)
Accuracy		(TP+TN)/(TP+TN+FP+FN)

TABLE 7.2 Basic parameters for the performance metrics

	Predicted age	
Actual age	**Above threshold**	**Below threshold**
Above threshold	True Positive (TP)	False Negative (FN)
Below threshold	False Positive (FP)	True Negative (TN)

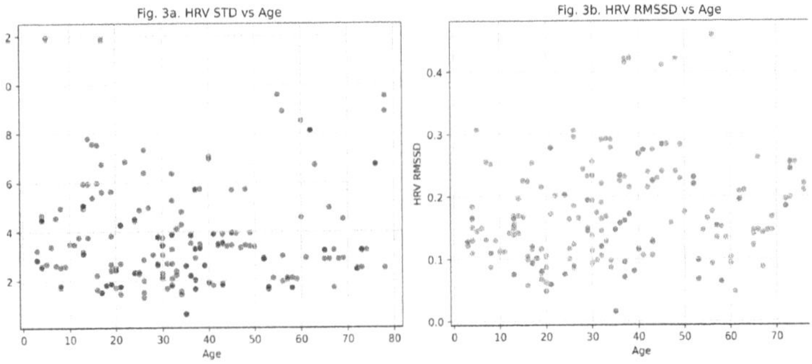

FIGURE 7.4 Age-related changes in heart rate variability

7.3 RESULTS

Age-Related Changes in Heart Rate Variability (HRV): Figure 7.4, which plots HRV STD and HRV RMSSD against age, reveals no definitive linear or easily interpretable pattern, despite clinical knowledge that Heart Rate Variability (HRV) generally declines with age. This discrepancy highlights a challenge: while population-level studies suggest age-related HRV trends, individual variability (e.g., lifestyle, genetics, or cardiac factors) often obscures clear patterns in real-world datasets. Traditional statistical methods or visualizations may fail to capture subtle, non-linear relationships or interactions between variables that influence HRV. This is where neural networks can help to identify hidden associations between age and ECG patterns.

Age estimation: Table 7.3 compares the age estimation performance—measured by Mean Absolute Error (MAE) across various feature-model combinations. The lowest MAE of 2.93 years was achieved using a feedforward neural network applied

TABLE 7.3 Age estimation result comparison between different methods and features

	Mean Absolute Error (MAE)			
Features	**LSTM**	**Inception1D**	**Feedforward Neural Network**	**Transformer Network**
De-noised ECG	3.06	3.03	2.93	4.71
PSD	4.61	5.09	4.34	5.69
Wavelet: sym4	3.96	3.61	3.34	4.83
Wavelet:db4	3.54	3.29	3.28	4.11
Wavelet: db1 to db4	3.82	3.75	3.71	4.61
Wavelet: db1 to db10	3.15	3.47	3.21	4.33
Wavelet: sym4, db1 to db10	3.21	3.12	3.00	3.86

to the de-noised ECG signal (illustrated in Figure 7.5). While models like LSTM and Inception1D produced results close to this, they did not surpass it. Power Spectral Density (PSD) offered no improvement, and wavelet-based methods yielded

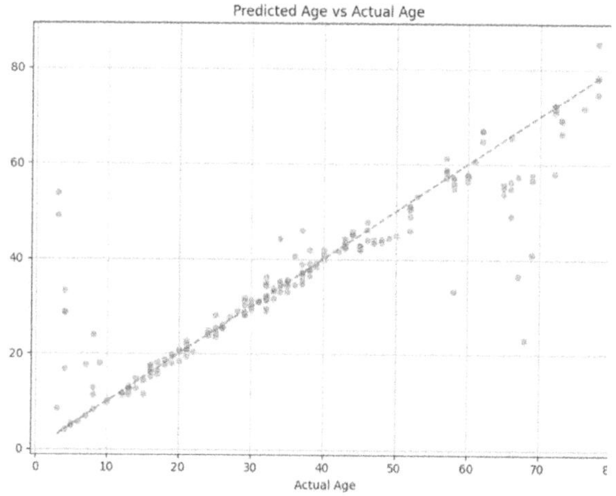

FIGURE 7.5 Predicted age vs. actual age, corresponding to the lowest MAE

performance comparable to the de-noised ECG. Overall, the use of extracted features did not lead to any notable performance gains across the evaluated models. These results were obtained through hyperparameter tuning on a significant scale, Table 7.3 presents a summary of the results obtained by using different algorithms and features.

In our overall dataset, 60.5% of participants were male (133 individuals) and 39.5% were female (87 individuals). For male participants, the model achieved a Mean Absolute Error (MAE) of 2.85. For female participants, the MAE was 3.06. Figures 7.6 and 7.7 demonstrate the plots of actual age against predicted age for male and female participants. No significant difference is observed between these two groups.

In recent years, different researchers have used transformer-based models for a wide range of ECG tasks, including arrhythmia classification and even age estimation. In this study, we implemented a transformer model incorporating multi-head

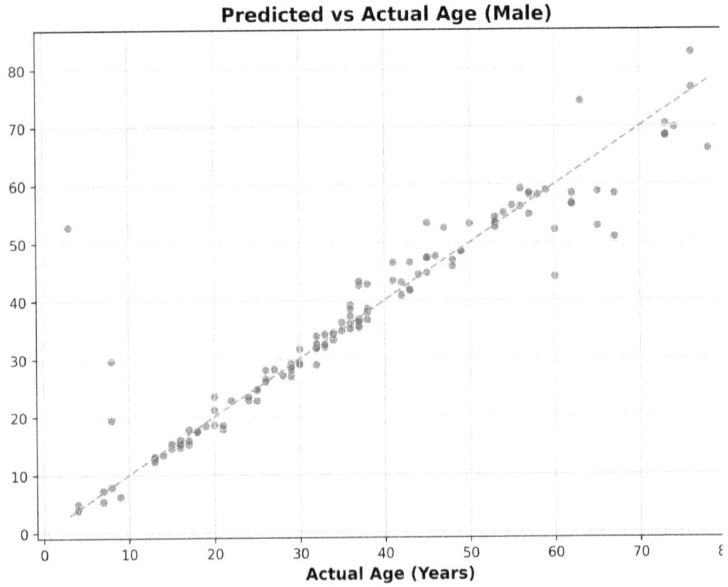

FIGURE 7.6 Predicted age vs. actual age, for male

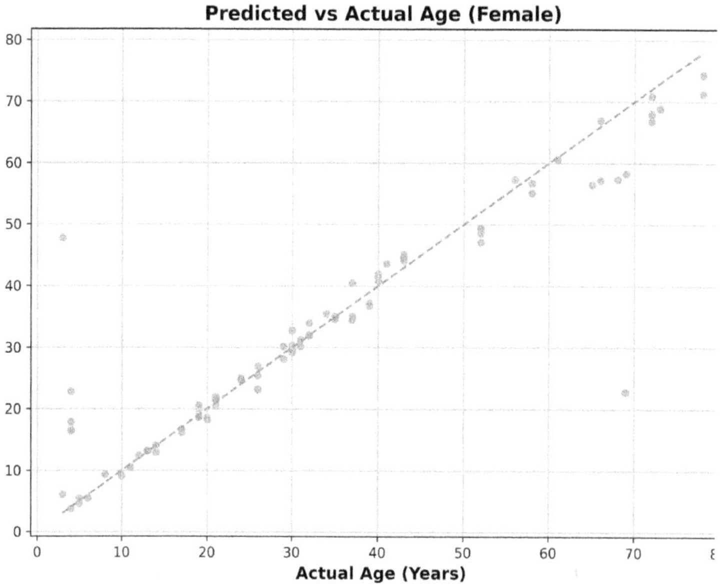

FIGURE 7.7 Predicted age vs. actual age, for female

self-attention, layer normalization, feedforward sublayers, and residual connections, followed by global average pooling. Interestingly, this approach did not yield better results compared to our baseline model.

Moreover, the processing time for transformers was significantly higher than that for FNN, LSTM, and Inception1D. This is expected, as transformers utilize more complex architectures with self-attention and multi-head mechanisms that substantially increase computational requirements compared to the more sequential and lightweight operations in FNN and other architectures. Table 7.4 presents the processing times for different methods and feature sets, as measured on a Google Colab Python 3 environment.

Transformers, with their self-attention mechanisms, usually outperform both CNNs and LSTMs in modeling long-range dependencies and capturing global signal context without succumbing to vanishing gradients. Attention mechanisms

TABLE 7.4 Processing time comparison across different methods and features

	Processing time (seconds)			
Features	**LSTM**	**Inception1D**	**Feedforward Neural Network**	**Transformer**
De-noised ECG	37.03	44.1	22.19	79.10
PSD	46.2	52.25	31.12	108.02
Wavelet: sym4	39.32	47.2	28.8	95.21
Wavelet:db4	39.1	46.93	29.03	95.44
Wavelet: db1 to db4	40.3	47.03	30.16	104.2
Wavelet: db1 to db10	40.7	47.11	30.22	111.19
Wavelet: sym4, db1 to db10	42.3	47.21	30.97	120.02

enable models to focus selectively on the most informative regions of ECG tracings, improving interpretability and predictive performance—especially as ECG datasets become larger. Nevertheless, transformer and attention-based methods typically demand more computational resources, larger datasets, and careful architectural design to avoid overfitting. In smaller-scale or resource-constrained scenarios with limited training data (as in this case—220 subjects, single-lead smartwatch ECG), the relative simplicity and data efficiency of FNN architectures can be advantageous and pragmatic.

Table 7.5 presents the age estimation performance across different age segments while using a feedforward neural network on de-noised ECG. Notably, the results were poorer for the 1–5 and 66–70-year groups, while the best performance was observed in the 11–15 and 16–20-year segments. The table also includes the total number of records (training and test data) for each segment to assess whether limited data size influenced performance. However, data scarcity does not appear to be a significant factor affecting the results. This trend aligns with clinical observations of how ECG characteristics change with

TABLE 7.5 Age estimation results for different age segments using a Feedforward Neural Network on the de-noised ECG

Age segment (years)	No. of total records	MAE	SD_{AE}	r
1–5	14	16.84	15.87	−0.56
6–10	10	2.85	3.84	0.60
11–15	19	0.84	0.43	0.85
16–20	24	0.86	0.46	0.82
21–25	14	1.18	0.86	0.57
26–30	17	1.05	0.89	0.72
31–35	25	1.10	0.64	0.84
36–40	22	1.54	1.69	0.62
41–45	15	1.09	0.75	0.80
46–50	6	2.45	1.24	0.26
51–55	16	3.48	1.09	0.77
56–60	10	1.79	2.73	−0.27
61–65	9	1.15	1.17	−0.49
66–70	5	15.30	11.04	−0.24
71–75	11	1.22	0.48	−0.08
76–80	3	6.25	4.74	0.90
Total	**220**	**2.93**	**6.2**	**0.94**

age [115–117]. Our hearts and nervous systems undergo significant changes in early adulthood, making these differences easier to detect. As we age, our heart rate variability (HRV) decreases rapidly at first, then more slowly, making it harder to pinpoint exact ages in older groups. It is important to note that while HRV decreases with age, resting heart rate itself tends to remain relatively stable or decrease only slightly in healthy adults. The more pronounced changes in HRV and other ECG features in younger adults contribute to more accurate age estimation for this group compared to older individuals. This result is further illustrated in Figure 7.5, which plots actual age against predicted age corresponding to the lowest MAE. Ideally, in the best-case scenario, the points should align closely with the 45-degree line, indicating perfect prediction. While the predictions remained consistent for most age groups, noticeable deviations were observed in the 1–10 and 60–70 year ranges.

The best MAE value of 2.93 from the Feedforward Neural Network was obtained in these hyperparameter settings: 2000 hidden layers and hidden units, learning rate of 0.005, batch size of 250, 200 epochs, and a dropout rate of 0.9. Figure 7.8 illustrates the optimization of hyperparameters for age estimation from de-noised ECG signals using FNN, LSTM, and Inception-1D models.

Figure 7.9 illustrates saliency maps derived from a feedforward neural network, highlighting the most influential features contributing to age prediction from de-noised ECG waveforms for samples representing eight distinct ages (3, 10, 20, 30, 40, 50, 60, and 70 years). Interestingly, the saliency patterns closely resemble the morphology of typical ECG signals. This alignment is compelling, as it demonstrates that the model's predictive focus corresponds with well-established physiological markers.

Table 7.6 presents a comparison of our age-estimation results with two recent studies conducted using clinical ECG data. Our study, based on smartwatch ECG signals, achieved significantly better performance. However, a limitation of our approach is that our dataset included only healthy individuals, whereas the other studies considered both healthy and non-healthy participants.

Table 7.7 presents a comparative analysis of age estimation performance between our method and an existing facial recognition-based age estimation solution [128]. Our ECG-based age estimation achieves a mean absolute error (MAE) of 2.93 years compared to 2.5 years for facial recognition methods.

Unlike facial recognition, ECG-based estimation shows no dependency on skin tone and supports privacy through on-device processing. Most importantly, it facilitates anonymized data handling. However, its accuracy can be affected by cardiovascular conditions, while facial recognition methods report no such health-related impact. While facial recognition often achieves high accuracy, it raises significant privacy concerns and

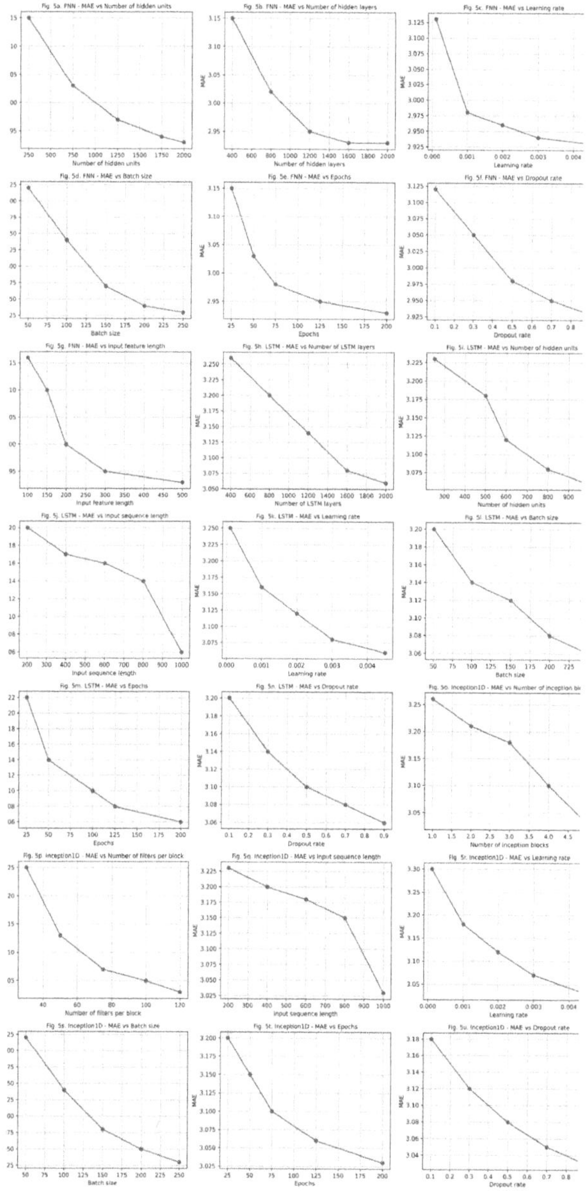

FIGURE 7.8 Optimizing hyperparameters for age estimation using FNN, LSTM, and Inception 1D models

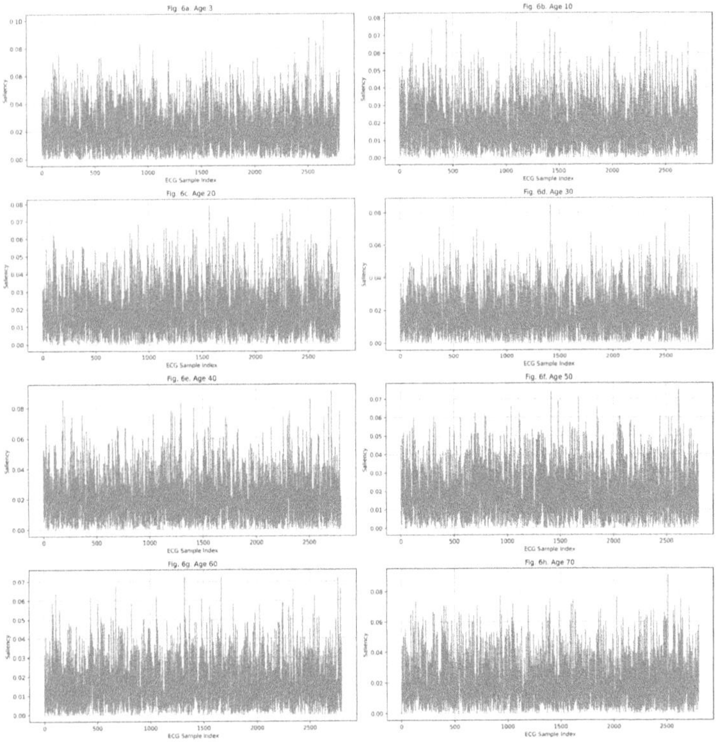

FIGURE 7.9 Saliency map revealing key ECG features for age prediction from de-noised ECG using FNN in different ages

can be susceptible to spoofing, lighting conditions, and demographic biases.

In contrast, ECG-based methods offer inherent liveness detection, are less intrusive, and are difficult to replicate or forge. Both approaches show minimal variation in performance across genders. Facial age estimation has been extensively validated across large-scale datasets, largely due to the wide availability of facial images. ECG-based age estimation, by comparison, is still an emerging field. In this study, our experiments were conducted on a limited number of samples. However, with broader access to ECG data—particularly from popular smartwatch manufacturers, this approach could be further validated

TABLE 7.6 Age estimation result comparison with other similar studies

Study	Data type	Methodology	MAE
Attia et al. [118]	Primary: Clinical ECG	CNN	≥7.0 (non-healthy) <7.0 (healthy)
Strodthoff et al. [122]	Secondary: PTB-XL database	Inception, RESNET, LSTM	7.12 (all) 6.80 (healthy) 7.37 (non-healthy)
Lima et al. [119]	Primary: Clinical ECG	CNN	≥8.0 (non-healthy) <8.0 (healthy)
Our method	Primary: Smartwatch ECG	Feedforward neural network	2.93 (healthy)

TABLE 7.7 Age estimation result comparison with other methods

Metrics	ECG-based (our study)	Facial recognition-based [128]
Accuracy (MAE)	2.93 years (data: 3 to 78 years)	2.5 years (data: 6 to 70 years)
Skin dependency	None observed	Varies with skin tone
Health impact	Significant	None reported
Anonymization	Ensures anonymity through biomedical data processing	Privacy concerns exist due to image data handling

and refined at scale, potentially offering a robust and privacy-preserving alternative for age estimation.

To address real-life needs, we performed binary classification within specific age ranges on the same dataset, using the mentioned models and features, based on age thresholds of 12 and 21 years. This method aims to classify whether the age output falls below or above these thresholds. The results are presented in Tables 7.8–7.10. These results were consistent across all models, which indicates the potential for this scheme to segregate adults and minors in accordance with real-life needs.

The Fitbit Sense Smartwatch is equipped with a low-power custom ARM Cortex processor designed primarily for

TABLE 7.8 Results of age classification using a Feedforward Neural Network on the de-noised ECG

Age	Acc	CI	TPR	TNR	FPR	FNR	PPV	NPV	F1
13	0.93	(0.85,1.00)	0.96	0.65	0.35	0.04	0.96	0.68	0.96
14	0.95	(0.89,1.00)	0.98	0.77	0.23	0.02	0.96	0.89	0.97
15	0.95	(0.89,1.00)	0.98	0.76	0.24	0.02	0.96	0.90	0.97
16	0.96	(0.90,1.00)	0.99	0.81	0.19	0.01	0.96	0.94	0.98
17	0.96	(0.90,1.00)	0.99	0.83	0.17	0.01	0.96	0.97	0.98
18	0.95	(0.89,1.00)	0.99	0.80	0.20	0.01	0.95	0.95	0.97
19	0.94	(0.87,1.00)	0.96	0.85	0.15	0.04	0.96	0.87	0.96
20	0.97	(0.92,1.00)	0.99	0.91	0.09	0.01	0.97	0.96	0.98
21	0.96	(0.90,1.00)	0.98	0.90	0.10	0.02	0.96	0.95	0.97

TABLE 7.9 Results of age classification using LSTM on the de-noised ECG

Age	Acc	CI	TPR	TNR	FPR	FNR	PPV	NPV	F1
13	0.94	(0.87,1.00)	0.97	0.65	0.35	0.03	0.96	0.75	0.97
14	0.95	(0.89,1.00)	0.99	0.74	0.26	0.01	0.96	0.92	0.97
15	0.96	(0.90,1.00)	1.00	0.76	0.24	0.00	0.96	1.00	0.98
16	0.95	(0.89,1.00)	0.98	0.78	0.22	0.02	0.96	0.9	0.97
17	0.94	(0.87,1.00)	0.98	0.78	0.22	0.02	0.95	0.91	0.97
18	0.94	(0.87,1.00)	0.98	0.82	0.18	0.02	0.95	0.90	0.97
19	0.94	(0.87,1.00)	0.96	0.87	0.13	0.04	0.96	0.87	0.96
20	0.95	(0.89,1.00)	0.96	0.91	0.09	0.04	0.97	0.89	0.97
21	0.94	(0.87,1.00)	0.96	0.90	0.10	0.04	0.96	0.90	0.96

TABLE 7.10 Results of age classification using INCEPTION 1D on the de-noised ECG

Age	Acc	CI	TPR	TNR	FPR	FNR	PPV	NPV	F1
13	0.93	(0.85,1.00)	0.95	0.74	0.26	0.05	0.97	0.65	0.96
14	0.96	(0.90,1.00)	0.99	0.81	0.19	0.01	0.97	0.93	0.98
15	0.96	(0.90,1.00)	0.98	0.85	0.15	0.02	0.97	0.91	0.99
16	0.96	(0.90,1.00)	0.98	0.86	0.14	0.02	0.97	0.91	0.98
17	0.96	(0.90,1.00)	0.97	0.9	0.10	0.03	0.98	0.88	0.97
18	0.96	(0.90,1.00)	0.98	0.89	0.11	0.02	0.97	0.99	0.97
19	0.96	(0.90,1.00)	0.97	0.91	0.09	0.03	0.98	0.90	0.97
20	0.96	(0.90,1.00)	0.96	0.94	0.06	0.04	0.98	0.89	0.97
21	0.96	(0.90,1.00)	0.97	0.93	0.07	0.03	0.97	0.92	0.97

energy-efficient health monitoring rather than high-performance computation. Its on-device processing capabilities are sufficient for basic real-time tasks such as heart rate variability (HRV) calculations and ECG signal filtering. However, more complex analyses, including arrhythmia detection or age prediction from ECG, need to be offloaded to a paired smartphone or cloud-based systems due to the device's limited computational resources.

Latency for simple operations remains low (around 10–100 milliseconds), enabling a smooth user experience for basic monitoring tasks. From a computational cost perspective, smart wearables perform lightweight processing on ECG signals such as noise reduction and compression. These preprocessing steps help reduce data size and transmission load, but the device does not handle resource-intensive operations like deep learning inference or statistical modeling. Those functions are executed off-device, preserving the wearable's processing and memory capacity.

In terms of battery usage, collecting ECG data has a relatively small but noticeable impact. A single ECG session, which typically lasts between 30 seconds and 2 minutes, uses a moderate amount of power primarily due to sensor activation and continuous Bluetooth transmission. While each session consumes only about 1–2% of the battery, regular use can shorten the device's average battery life from around six days to approximately three to four days depending on frequency and other concurrent sensor usage [129].

Regarding data security and anonymization, Fitbit uses Bluetooth Low Energy (BLE) protocols with encryption to securely transmit ECG data to the user's paired smartphone. Once uploaded, the data is stored in the Fitbit cloud, now operated by Google, where it is protected through end-to-end encryption. For research and analytics purposes, Fitbit de-identifies health data in compliance with regulations like the General Data Protection Regulation (GDPR) and the Health Insurance

Portability and Accountability Act (HIPAA). This means that any personally identifiable information (PII) is stripped from datasets before analysis or third-party sharing [129, 130].

The transferability of our ECG-based machine learning model, from data acquired using the Fitbit Sense to other consumer-grade wearable devices, is influenced by multiple hardware and signal processing factors, though not all have equal impact. Electrode configuration and signal quality tend to be less critical barriers, especially for wrist-worn wearable applications. Most consumer wearables use similar single-lead, wrist-based setups, which means ECG morphology remains broadly comparable across devices. Variations in signal quality due to skin contact or minor hardware noise can typically be addressed through standard preprocessing techniques for artifact removal. However, substantial differences, such as a shift from wrist to chest-based electrode placement or significantly increased noise, can affect model generalizability unless addressed through retraining.

In contrast, sampling rate is a more significant constraint. A model trained on Fitbit Sense data may lose accuracy and introduce bias when applied to signals captured at lower sampling rates, as certain waveform features may be lost or distorted. While higher sampling rates offer richer data, they can also introduce additional noise and increase the demand for more advanced filtering. Therefore, frequency filtering and signal preprocessing must be carefully tailored to the specific sampling characteristics of each device [131, 132]. A summary outlining these factors is provided in Table 7.11.

Modern wearable devices, including smartwatches and fitness trackers—have steadily improved in computational capability, making on-device inference for biomedical signals like ECG both feasible and increasingly relevant for real-world deployment. While the current study performs model inference off-device, discussing strategies for moving toward lightweight, on-device models would enhance the practical impact and future orientation of this research.

TABLE 7.11 Key factors impacting model transferability across different devices

Factor	Impact on model transferability
Sampling rate	Alters signal resolution and information; hence the model needs to be carefully adapted.
Electrode configuration	For any single-lead ECG device, ECG morphology remains broadly comparable with some minor adjustment in the model.
Signal noise	Affects signal's reliability; can be mitigated through preprocessing without any major change in the model.

To facilitate real-time, privacy-preserving age estimation directly on wearable devices, model compression techniques such as pruning, quantization, and knowledge distillation offer promising solutions. Pruning eliminates redundant model parameters, significantly reducing computational and memory requirements without substantial accuracy loss. Quantization compresses model weights and activations to lower numerical precision, further decreasing the model's size and enabling efficient inference on device-specific hardware [131, 132]. These approaches have recently enabled robust ECG algorithms to run in real-time on commercial wearable devices. We anticipate that applying these strategies to our models will enable a seamless transition from research-grade, off-device inference to end-to-end wearable solutions in future work.

Developing an accurate, secure, easily deployable, and anonymous biometric-based age estimation system remains a significant challenge. Despite certain limitations, the electrocardiogram (ECG) shows considerable promise, especially when integrated into accessible platforms such as smartwatch-based ECG applications. To the best of our knowledge, this study is among the first to explore age estimation using ECG signals collected from smartwatches. Although our data set was limited in size and included only healthy subjects, the promising results for both age estimation and age verification highlight the potential for further research in this area. We compared here the effectiveness of various features and machine learning algorithms to identify an optimal approach.

Interestingly, a simplified model using the original de-noised ECG signal outperformed more complex, feature-based models. This is likely due to the data set comprising only healthy individuals. While this approach may seem technically less sophisticated, it offers significant advantages for real-world applications, enabling easier implementation and faster processing on devices like smart wearables. Overall, the encouraging results from this study provide a strong foundation for future experimentation and the potential real-world deployment of ECG-based age verification technology.

CHAPTER 8

Conclusion

From the earliest reliance on physical identity documents to today's complex digital ecosystems, the evolution of age verification reflects a broader co-evolution between technology, regulation, and societal expectations. What began as a localized and manual process has transformed into critical technical infrastructure embedded across the global digital environment. Each phase along this journey has expanded not only technical capability but also expectations around safety, accountability, and user rights.

Age verification has expanded well beyond its original function of restricting access to age-inappropriate content. It now sits at the intersection of social media governance, child online safety, digital identity systems, data protection law, and platform accountability. In this broader context, age verification is no longer a discrete compliance mechanism but a foundational component of digital trust infrastructure.

Across jurisdictions, the central policy question has shifted from whether to implement age verification to how it should be designed, governed, and enforced. This transition has intensified scrutiny of privacy risks, particularly those related to identity disclosure and data collection. In response, privacy-enhancing

DOI: 10.1201/9781003643517-8

approaches are gaining traction. These have led to a wave of technical innovation, standards development, and platform integration.

For successful age verification, technical feasibility alone is insufficient. Public trust depends equally on security, transparency, and demonstrable resilience. The European Union's trial rollout of a dedicated age verification application in April 2026 is one such example. While it represents a significant step toward standardization, early reports of vulnerabilities and hacking allegations highlight a persistent structural challenge—the gap between regulatory ambition and operational robustness.

Equally significant is the shift toward distributed responsibility. Modern frameworks increasingly allocate obligations across multiple actors, including platforms, device manufacturers, app stores, and payment providers. However, this distribution remains actively contested between device-level and platform-level approaches, as each side continues to push the responsibility to the other side. Companies such as Apple and Google prefer platform-level solutions. Platforms and content providers, such as Meta and Aylo, advocate for age verification at device, operating system, or App store layers. This tension reflects deeper questions about control, responsibility, and liability.

Market responses further illustrate the real-world impact of regulatory design. In several jurisdictions, stringent age verification requirements have prompted major adult-content platforms to withdraw services, citing concerns over privacy risks, compliance costs, and technical feasibility.

However, early evidence from large-scale deployments of age verification in 2025–2026 (in the United Kingdom, Australia, and Malaysia) shows encouraging signs. Both the technical effectiveness and social impact of these implementations are becoming more evident, supported by qualitative and quantitative findings. As a result, a broader public acceptance of age verification is clearly visible in those countries.

Looking ahead, interoperability is emerging as a key priority in the age verification framework. Leading players in the age verification industry are developing interoperable platforms capable of supporting multiple providers and solutions. The push toward standardized, cross-border systems is accelerating.

Despite this progress, implementation remains uneven. Differences in legal systems, constitutional frameworks, and cultural attitudes toward privacy continue to shape adoption across regions. Governance structures add further complexity. For example, the United States relies on state-level variation, the European Union combines shared principles with individual country-wise implementation, and Canada emphasizes provincial flexibility.

Debates around privacy and data protection also continue. In the United States, courts are examining whether mandatory age verification imposes disproportionate limits on freedom of expression. In Europe and Canada, regulators focus more on proportionality, necessity, and compliance with data protection laws.

Issues of exclusion, accessibility, and potential discrimination also persist, particularly for users without access to identity documents or compatible technologies. These concerns highlight the importance of designing systems that are not only effective and privacy-preserving but also inclusive and equitable.

Technological innovation continues rapidly. Alongside established methods such as ID verification and facial analysis, newer approaches such as behavioral biometrics, voice analysis, hand gesture recognition, and electrocardiogram are emerging. However, real-world evaluations consistently show that no single method is universally reliable. This reinforces the belief that effective age assurance requires hybrid and multilayered approaches.

Crucially, there is growing recognition that age verification alone cannot ensure comprehensive child protection. It must be complemented by broader measures, including algorithmic accountability, content moderation, safer platform design, and parental controls.

Taken together, these developments position age verification as a central element of modern digital governance. It is not only a regulatory tool but also part of digital identity infrastructure, a site of technological and commercial competition, and a test case for balancing child protection with fundamental rights. The debate is no longer just about restricting access—it is about how responsibility, risk, and trust are distributed across the digital ecosystem.

Moving forward, progress will depend on advancing privacy-preserving technologies, developing interoperable solutions, and maintaining adaptive regulatory frameworks. It will require sustained collaboration among regulators, industry, researchers, and broader stakeholders, including activists, educators, parents, and users. Ultimately, age verification should be understood not as a static compliance requirement, but as an evolving governance challenge at the intersection of child protection, technology, market forces, and fundamental human needs.

Appendix

A Chronology of Age Verification

1215: The Magna Carta in England establishes foundational legal protections and enforces 21 as the age of full legal responsibility under common law, a benchmark later adopted across British colonies and influencing modern age thresholds.

1272–1307: Under Edward I, English common law further formalizes 21 as the age of majority for contracts, land ownership, and independent legal action.

1923: The United Kingdom strengthens alcohol regulations by prohibiting the sale of alcohol to individuals under 18, helping normalize age checks for restricted goods.

1931: Nevada legalizes casino gambling with a minimum age of 21, aligning age restrictions with alcohol laws and formalizing verification in high-risk commercial sectors.

1960s: US states increasingly require proof of age for alcohol purchases, making ID-based verification a standard retail practice.

1971: The US ratifies the 26th Amendment, lowering the voting age to 18 while many states later restore alcohol laws to 21, reinforcing differentiated age thresholds across civic and commercial domains.

1984: The United States effectively standardizes 21 as the legal drinking age nationwide.

1989: The UN Convention on the Rights of the Child defines a child as anyone under 18, establishing a global standard .

1990: The World Wide Web becomes publicly accessible, enabling widespread digital content distribution and creating future demand for online age assurance mechanisms.

1998: The United States enacts COPPA (Children's Online Privacy Protection Act), requiring verifiable parental consent for collecting data from children under 13 and establishing the first major legal framework for online age verification.

2000: COPPA comes into force, shaping global platform policies and leading most social media services to adopt 13 as the minimum user age.

2004: Facebook launches with a 13+ age requirement aligned with COPPA, relying on self-declared birthdates rather than robust verification.

2007: Pornhub launched in Montreal, accelerating access to user-generated adult content .

2010–2019: Widespread broadband and smartphone adoption make streaming adult content widely available, intensifying concern over youth exposure.

2011: Snapchat launches with a 13+ policy, continuing industry reliance on self-declaration instead of verified age assurance.

2017: TikTok expands globally, rapidly becoming one of the most widely used youth platforms while relying on self-reported age.

March 2020: On the International Women's Day (March 8), protesters gather outside Pornhub HQ in Montreal , decrying child access to porn and calling for third-party age verification.

December 2020: A New York Times investigation reveals large volumes of child sexual abuse material and non-consensual content on Pornhub, prompting removal of unverified videos and payment processor (Visa/Mastercard) withdrawal.

December 2020: Mastercard and VISA suspended all transactions with Pornhub, citing audit findings of unlawful content.

2020–2021: Canadian parliamentary committees investigate Pornhub, concluding moderation failures and recommending mandatory, independent age verification mechanisms.

2021: Canada introduces Bill S-210 (Protecting Young Persons from Exposure to Pornography Act), marking a shift toward legislated age verification for adult content.

2023: Multiple US states (including Louisiana, Texas, and Utah) pass laws requiring age verification for adult websites, marking the first large-scale enforcement wave in the United States.

October 2023: The UK Online Safety Act becomes a law, imposing detailed responsibilities on online services to safeguard users, including age verification requirements for certain content.

April 2024: The first Global Age Assurance Standards Summit is held in Manchester, convening regulators, technologists, and civil society to advance privacy-preserving age verification .

December 2024: Australia passes amendments to its online safety framework proposing strict age assurance obligations.

April 2025: The second Global Age Assurance Standards Summit takes place in Amsterdam, focusing on interoperability, privacy safeguards, and scalable age assurance models.

July 2025: The UK begins full enforcement of age verification requirements for commercial pornography websites under the Online Safety Act.

October 2025: Pornhub partially restricts services in the UK in response to strict age verification compliance requirements.

December 2025: Discord and Roblox begin deploying facial age estimation and behavioral age inference tools across their platforms, extending age verification into virtual environments.

December 2025: Australia enforces mass-scale age verification by restricting social media access for users under 16.

January–December 2025: Over a dozen US states expand age verification mandates beyond pornography to include social media and app stores.

March 2026: Indonesia becomes the first Asian country to restrict social media access for users under 16.

April 2026: The Senate of Canada approves Bill S-209 as a renewed legislative effort to mandate age verification for sexually explicit online material following earlier stalled bills.

April 2026: The ruling Liberal Party of Canada adopted a motion to restrict under-16 access to social media and generative AI. Following this, the Minister of Canadian Heritage emphasized the issue as a serious policy priority.

April 2026: The European Commission announced their new age verification app.

April 2026: The Third Global Age Assurance Standards Summit concluded in Manchester, highlighting real-world success stories from large-scale deployments.

Glossary

ACCS (Age Check Certification Scheme) (UK, 2019): A certification program that evaluates age assurance providers against defined standards for accuracy, privacy, and reliability.

Age Assurance (2010s–): An umbrella term for processes used to determine or confirm a user's age or age range at varying levels of confidence.

Age Estimation (2010s–): The process of predicting an individual's exact age or a narrowly defined age value.

Age Verification (2010s–): The process of confirming that an individual meets a specified age threshold (e.g., under 13, 13+, 18+).

Anonymity-Preserving Age Verification (2020s–): An approach to age verification that confirms the age range without revealing a user's identity.

Audiovisual Media Services Directive (AVMSD) (European Union, 2018): A directive regulating audiovisual media that requires measures to protect minors, including age-based access restrictions.

Aylo (formerly MindGeek) (2004-): A major operator of online adult content platforms, frequently referenced in debates on age verification and platform responsibility.

Bill S-209/Bill S-210 (Canada, 2021–): Canadian Senate bills proposing mandatory age verification for access to sexually explicit online content.

Browser-Level Age Verification (2020s–): A proposed model in which web browsers facilitate or enforce age checks across websites.

CAN DGSI 127:2025 (Canada, 2025): A Canadian standard providing guidance for the design and implementation of age assurance systems.

Child Rights Impact Assessment (CRIA) (2010s–): A framework used to evaluate how policies or technologies affect children's rights and well-being.

COPPA (Children's Online Privacy Protection Act) (United States, 1998): A US law regulating online data collection from children under 13, requiring verifiable parental consent.

Data Minimization: A principle requiring that only the minimum necessary personal data be collected for a specific purpose.

Device-Level/Operating System-Level Age Verification (2020s–): An approach that integrates age assurance into devices or operating systems rather than individual platforms.

Digital Child and Adolescent Statute (Brazil, 2020): A proposed legal framework that includes requirements for age verification for access to certain online content.

Digital Services Act (DSA) (European Union, 2022): A regulation requiring online platforms to address systemic risks, including protecting minors through proportionate safeguards.

EU Age Verification Blueprint (European Union, 2026): A technical framework outlining privacy-preserving methods for implementing age verification systems.

EU Digital Identity Wallet (European Union, 2024–2025): A system enabling users to store and present verified identity attributes, including proof of age.

Face Analysis Technology Evaluation (FATE) (National Institute of Standards and Technology, 2024–): A benchmarking program evaluating the performance of face analysis systems, including age verification technologies.

General Data Protection Regulation (GPRD) (European Union, 2016): A comprehensive data protection law requiring privacy safeguards such as data minimization and privacy-by-design.

German Youth Media Protection Act (JMStV) (Germany, 2020): : A legal framework requiring age controls for content deemed harmful to minors.

Harmful to Minors (HTM) (United States): A legal classification for content considered inappropriate or harmful to individuals under the age of majority.

IEEE 2089.1 (IEEE, 2024): A standard specifying requirements for online age verification systems, emphasizing privacy, proportionality, and interoperability.

ISO/IEC 27566-1:2025 (ISO/IEC, 2025): An international standard providing guidance on privacy-preserving age assurance.

ISOC Age Restriction Principles (Internet Society, 2020): Guidelines promoting effective and rights-respecting approaches to age restrictions online.

IT Rules 2021 (India, 2021): Regulations establishing obligations for online platforms, including measures to protect children from harmful content.

Mean Absolute Error (MAE): A measure used in age estimation to represent the average difference between predicted and actual age.

Online Criminal Harms Act (Singapore, 2023): A law requiring platforms to mitigate online harms, including restricting access to harmful content.

Online Safety Act (United Kingdom, 2023): A law imposing detailed responsibilities on online services to safeguard users, including age verification requirements for certain content.

Online Safety Amendment Act (Australia, 2024): A law establishing minimum age requirements for social media use and mandating enforcement mechanisms.

PIPEDA (Personal Information Protection and Electronic Documents Act) (Canada, 2000): Canada's federal privacy law governing the collection and use of personal information.

Privacy-by-Design (1990s-): A principle requiring privacy protections to be built into systems from the outset.

Proportionality (2010s–): The principle that age assurance measures should align with the level of risk and potential harm.

SREN Law (France, 2024): A law mandating age verification for access to pornographic websites.

Token-Based Age Verification (2020s–): A method using reusable digital tokens to confirm age eligibility without repeated data sharing.

Youth Protection Act (South Korea, 2020): A law requiring age verification for access to certain online content, including adult material and gaming.

References

1. Chicago Center for Torah Learning. (n.d.). *Shabbos 056*. Chicago Center for Torah Learning. https://www.thechicagocenter.org/
2. Janes, J. (n.d.). The age of legal maturity in Biblical law. *Journal of the Ancient Near Eastern Society.* https://janes.jtsa.edu/volumes/21/1/article-2/
3. Mark Cole. (2025). *Why the age 30 is so significant in the Bible.* https://www.markcole.ca/why-the-age-30-is-so-significant-in-the-bible/
4. Got Questions Ministries. (2022). *How old were Jesus' disciples?* https://www.gotquestions.org/how-old-were-Jesus-disciples.html
5. Encyclopaedia.com. (n.d.). *Age of majority.* Encyclopedia.com. https://www.encyclopedia.com/law/encyclopedias-almanacs-transcripts-and-maps/age-majority
6. Holt, J. C. (1992). *Magna Carta* (2nd ed.). Cambridge University Press.
7. Legislation.gov.uk. (2011). *Statute of Westminster, The First (1275).* https://www.legislation.gov.uk/aep/Edw1/3/5
8. Pollock, F., & Maitland, F. W. (1895). *The history of English law before the time of Edward I (Vol. 1).* Cambridge University Press.
9. Encyclopaedia Britannica. (2025). *Age of majority: Common law traditions.* https://www.britannica.com/topic/age-of-majority
10. National WWII Museum. (2020, October 27). *"Old enough to fight, old enough to vote": The WWII roots of the 26th amendment.* https://www.nationalww2museum.org/war/articles/voting-age-26th-amendment
11. Murrill, B. J. (2025, April 23). *The twenty-sixth amendment and reduction of the voting age (Part 1): Introduction* (Legal Sidebar No. LSB11286). Congressional Research Service. https://www.congress.gov/crs_external_products/LSB/PDF/LSB11286/LSB11286.3.pdf

12. *Family Law Reform Act 1969.* (1969). Legislation.gov.uk. https://www.legislation.gov.uk/ukpga/1969/46
13. Légifrance. (1974). *Loi n° 74-631 du 5 juillet 1974 fixant à dix-huit ans l'âge de la majorité.* https://www.legifrance.gouv.fr/loda/id/JORFTEXT000000700039/
14. Nippon.com. (2022, April 1). *Official age of adulthood in Japan lowered to 18.* https://www.nippon.com/en/japan-data/h01285/
15. United Nations. (1989). *Convention on the Rights of the Child. United Nations.* https://www.un.org/en/about-us/universal-declaration-of-human-rights
16. World Population Review. (2026). *Age of majority by country 2026.* https://worldpopulationreview.com/country-rankings/age-of-majority-by-country
17. Library of Congress. (2023, November 19). *100-year anniversary of restrictions on alcohol in England and Wales for those under 18.* https://blogs.loc.gov/law/2023/11/100-year-anniversary-of-restrictions-on-alcohol-in-england-and-wales-for-those-under-18/
18. Day in Wine History. (n.d.). *A history of minimum legal drinking age limits.* https://thisdayinwinehistory.com/a-history-of-minimum-legal-drinking-age-limits/
19. Klitzner, A. L., Zerhouni, R. D., & Gregory, M. D. (1996). The minimum legal drinking age: History, effectiveness, and ongoing debate. *Journal of Studies on Alcohol*, 57(6), 581–589. https://pmc.ncbi.nlm.nih.gov/articles/PMC6876521
20. Bachman, C. M., et al. (2015). Minimum ages of legal access for tobacco in the United States and the relationship with early-onset smoking. *American Journal of Public Health,* e15–e20. https://pmc.ncbi.nlm.nih.gov/articles/PMC4902755
21. U.S. Food and Drug Administration. "*Tobacco 21*". https://www.fda.gov/tobacco-products/retail-sales-tobacco-products/tobacco-21
22. DigitalRG. *Minimum gambling age and why regulators believe it is important.* https://digitalrg.com/blog/minimum-gambling-age-and-why-regulators-believe-it-is-important
23. GamblingMaps.org. (2026). *Legal gambling age by country 2026: Per-vertical breakdown.* https://gamblingmaps.org/map/regulations/legal-age

24. Government of Canada. (2018). *Cannabis Act (S.C. 2018, c. 16)*. Justice Laws Website. https://laws-lois.justice.gc.ca/eng/acts/c-24.5/
25. Science and Media Museum. (2020). *A short history of the internet*. https://www.scienceandmediamuseum.org.uk/objects-and-stories/short-history-internet
26. Federal Trade Commission. (2025). *Children's Online Privacy Protection Rule (COPPA)*. https://www.ftc.gov/legal-library/browse/rules/childrens-online-privacy-protection-rule-coppa
27. Pew Research Center. (2025). *Social media fact sheet*. https://www.pewresearch.org/internet/fact-sheet/social-media/
28. Cybernews. (2025). *Social media age restrictions: A comprehensive list*. https://cybernews.com/editorial/mature-content-online
29. Our World in Data. (2019). *The rise of social media*. https://ourworldindata.org/rise-of-social-media
30. Cybernews. (2025). *Social media age restrictions: A comprehensive list*. https://cybernews.com/editorial/mature-content-online/
31. Saunders, R. (2024). Big data on Pornhub insights: Datafication and the making of the online pornography industry. *Convergence: The International Journal of Research into New Media Technologies*, 30(5), 1–17. https://journals.sagepub.com/doi/abs/10.1177/13548565251363693
32. MacDonald, M. (2019). *Desire for data: PornHub and the platformization of a culture industry*. Concordia University. https://spectrum.library.concordia.ca/986147/
33. Netflix Tudum. (2023, March 15). *Netflix Pornhub documentary history: How did porn videos start?* https://www.netflix.com/tudum/articles/pornhub-history-legal-timeline
34. CBC News. (2024, April 3). *Pornhub changed the world, but its empire faces a reckoning*. https://www.cbc.ca/news/business/pornhub-empire-adult-industry-1.7157843
35. Shead, S. (2025, January 24). *Exclusive: U.S. whistleblower says Mastercard, Visa failed to stop payments on child sex abuse material*. Reuters. https://www.reuters.com/world/us/us-whistleblower-says-mastercard-visa-failed-stop-payments-child-sex-abuse-2025-01-24/

36. Top Class Actions. (2025, April 29). *Judge grants class certification to Pornhub child pornography victims.* https://topclassactions.com/lawsuit-settlements/lawsuit-news/class-action-lawsuit-alleges-pornhub-encouraged-child-pornography/
37. Federal Trade Commission. (2025, September 3). *FTC takes action against operators of Pornhub and other pornographic sites deceiving users about efforts.* https://www.ftc.gov/news-events/news/press-releases/2025/09/ftc-takes-action-against-operators-pornhub-other-pornographic-sites-deceiving-users-about-efforts
38. Kristof, N. D. (2020, December 4). *The children of Pornhub.* The New York Times. https://www.nytimes.com/2020/12/04/opinion/sunday/pornhub-rape-trafficking.html
39. Mastercard. (2020, December 9). *Mastercard, Visa end card use on Pornhub amid controversy.* CBC News. https://www.cbc.ca/news/canada/montreal/mastercard-ends-card-use-on-pornhub-1.5836289
40. Radio-Canada Ombudsman. (2021, September 17). *Review by the Radio-Canada Ombudsman of a complaint regarding the article "Une croisade chrétienne pour fermer Pornhub"* [Ombudsman review]. https://site-cbc.radio-canada.ca/media/6302/re-vision-rafaela-diaz-17-septembre-2021-anglais.pdf
41. CTV News. (2020, March 5). *Protest planned in front of Pornhub HQ in Montreal on International Women's Day.* CTV News. https://www.ctvnews.ca/montreal/article/protesters-demonstrate-in-front-of-pornhub-hq-in-montreal-on-international-womens-day/
42. Standing Committee on Access to Information, Privacy and Ethics. (2021, June 17). *Committee news release – June 17, 2021 – ETHI (43-2): Standing Committee on Access to Information, Privacy and Ethics publishes report on the protection of privacy and reputation on platforms such as Pornhub* [News release]. Parliament of Canada. https://www.ourcommons.ca/documentviewer/en/43-2/ETHI/news-release/11429823
43. Office of the Privacy Commissioner of Canada. (2024). *Briefing note: Appearance before the Standing Senate Committee on Legal and Constitutional Affairs on Bill S-203 (Protecting Young Persons from Exposure to Pornography Act).* https://www.priv.gc.ca/en/privacy-and-transparency-at-the-opc/proactive-disclosure/opc-parl-bp/secu_20240527/bn-s203_20240527/?id=7777-6-629988

44. Office of the Privacy Commissioner of Canada. (2024). *Investigation into Aylo (formerly MindGeek)'s compliance with PIPEDA in relation to image-based abuse on Pornhub.com and other adult sites.* https://www.priv.gc.ca/en/opc-actions-and-decisions/investigations/investigations-into-businesses/2024/pipeda-2024-001/
45. Bill S-210, *An Act to restrict young persons' online access to sexually explicit material*, 44th Parliament, 1st Session, Parliament of Canada, Ottawa, ON, Canada, Nov. 2021–Apr. 2023. [Online]. Available: https://www.parl.ca/legisinfo/en/bill/44-1/s-210
46. Bill S-209, *An Act to restrict young persons' online access to pornographic material* (Protecting Young Persons from Exposure to Pornography Act), 45th Parliament, 1st Session, Parliament of Canada, Ottawa, ON, Canada, May 2025–present. [Online]. Available: https://www.parl.ca/legisinfo/en/bill/45-1/s-209
47. European Parliament. (2025). *Press release on new EU digital youth protections and age limits.* https://www.europarl.europa.eu/news/en/press-room/20251120IPR31496
48. European Parliament. (2025, November 20). *Press release: Children should be at least 16 to access social media, say MEPs.* European Parliament. https://www.europarl.europa.eu/news/en/press-room/20251120IPR31496
49. CBS News. (2022, September 30). *U.K. coroner: Social media contributed to Molly Russell's suicide.* CBS News. https://www.cbsnews.com/news/molly-russell-suicide-death-coroner-social-media-instagram-pinterest/
50. CBS News. (2021, October 4). *Facebook whistleblower Frances Haugen: "The thing I saw at Facebook over and over again....* https://www.cbsnews.com/news/facebook-whistleblower-frances-haugen-misinformation-public-60-minutes-2021-10-03/
51. Australian Government. (2024). *Online Safety Amendment (Social Media Minimum Age) Act 2024* (C2024A00127). https://www.legislation.gov.au/C2024A00127/asmade/details
52. Australian Government. (2025). *Age Assurance Technology Trial: Final Report. Commonwealth of Australia.* https://www.twobirds.com/en/insights/2025/australia/age-assurance-technology-trial-summary-and-implications-for-online-safety
53. Australian eSafety Commissioner. (2025). *Social media age restrictions.* https://www.esafety.gov.au/about-us/industry-regulation/social-media-age-restrictions

54. Reuters. (2026, January 26). *French Assembly approves social media ban for under-15s.* https://www.lemonde.fr/en/france/article/2026/01/27/french-lawmakers-approve-social-media-ban-for-under-15s_6749844_7.html
55. GovFacts. (2025). *U.S. social media regulations for minors.* https://govfacts.org/tech-innovation/digital-rights-privacy/online-child-safety/u-s-social-media-regulations-for-minors/
56. *Online Safety Act 2023.* (2023). Legislation.gov.uk. https://www.legislation.gov.uk/ukpga/2023/50
57. European Commission. (2025). *Digital Services Act* (DSA). https://commission.europa.eu/strategy-and-policy/priorities-2019-2024/europe-fit-digital-age/digital-services-act_en
58. Reuters. (2025). *Five EU states to test age verification app to protect children.* https://www.reuters.com/sustainability/boards-policy-regulation/five-eu-states-test-age-verification-app-protect-children-2025-07-14/
59. Exploding Topics. (2025). *How many gamers are there?* https://explodingtopics.com/blog/number-of-gamers
60. UNICEF. (2025). *Protecting children in online gaming.* https://www.unicef.org/innocenti/media/11836/file/UNICEF-Innocenti-Protecting-Children-Online-Gaming-Working-Paper-2025.pdf
61. Canadian Centre for Child Protection. (2026). *Extreme online violence targeting girls on the rise.* https://www.protectchildren.ca/en/press-and-media/news-releases/2026/extreme-violence
62. ABC News. (2026). *Siblings rescued after alleged kidnapping by 19-year-old they met online.* Good Morning America. https://abcnews.go.com/GMA/News/siblings-rescued-after-alleged-kidnapping-19-year-met/story?id=129794514
63. Wired. (2025). *Roblox's AI-powered age verification is a complete mess.* https://www.wired.com/story/robloxs-ai-powered-age-verification-is-a-complete-mess/
64. BBC. (2025). *ID photos of 70,000 users may have been leaked, Discord says.* https://www.bbc.com/news/articles/c8jmzd972leo
65. CNN Business. (2025). *After a wave of lawsuits, Character.AI will no longer let minors use its app.* https://www.cnn.com/2025/10/29/tech/character-ai-teens-under-18-app-changes
66. Stability AI. (2025). *New safeguards for minors on Stable Diffusion.* Stability AI Newsroom. https://stability.ai/news/minor-safeguards-stable-diffusion

67. The New York Times. (2025). *Character.AI to bar children under 18 from using its chatbots*. https://www.nytimes.com/2025/10/29/technology/characterai-underage-users.html
68. Canadian Broadcasting Corporation (CBC). (2026). *Liberal Party vote on social media age restrictions*. https://www.cbc.ca/news/politics/liberal-party-vote-on-social-media-age-restrictions-9.7159746
69. Global News. (2026). *Ottawa is very seriously considering a youth social media ban*. https://globalnews.ca/news/11803954/ottawa-very-seriously-considering-youth-social-media-ban
70. Centre for Information Policy Leadership. (2024). *Age assurance & age verification laws in the United States*. https://www.informationpolicycentre.com/
71. National Conference of State Legislatures. (2025). *Online age verification and social media laws by state*. https://www.ncsl.org/technology-and-communication/social-media-and-age-verification-laws
72. Congressional Research Service. (2024). *Kids Online Safety Act (KOSA): Overview and policy considerations*. https://crsreports.congress.gov/product/pdf/IF/IF12409
73. European Commission. (2025). *The age verification manual: EU Digital Identity Wallet technical specifications*. https://ec.europa.eu/digital-building-blocks/sites/spaces/EUDIGITALIDENTITYWALLET/pages/930450954/The+Age+Verification+Manual
74. Better Internet for Kids. (2024). *Law No. 2024-449 of 21 May 2024 aimed at securing and regulating the digital space*. https://better-internet-for-kids.europa.eu/en/rules-guidelines/law-no-2024-449-may-21-2024-aimed-securing-and-regulating-digital-space
75. German Commission for Youth Media Protection (KJM). (2021). *Youth Media Protection State Treaty (JMStV): Age protection rules in digital media*. https://www.kjm-online.de/fileadmin/user_upload/Rechtsgrundlagen/Gesetze_Staatsvertraege/JMStV/JMStV_english_version.pdf
76. Media Commission Ireland. (2024). *Online Safety Code*. https://www.cnam.ie/online-safety-code/
77. European Commission. (2026, April 15). *European age verification app to keep children safe online*. https://commission.europa.eu/news-and-media/news/european-age-verification-app-keep-children-safe-online-2026-04-15_en

78. UK Government. (2019). *Online Harms White Paper.* https://www.gov.uk/government/consultations/online-harms-white-paper
79. UK Government. (2021). *Online Safety Bill: Explanatory Notes.* https://assets.publishing.service.gov.uk/media/609a6ee1d3bf7f28890dab48/Explanatory_Notes_Accessible.pdf
80. UK Government. (2023). *Online Safety Act.* https://www.gov.uk/government/collections/online-safety-act
81. Australian Government. (2024). *Online Safety Amendment (Social Media Minimum Age) Act 2024.* https://www.infrastructure.gov.au/media-communications/internet/online-safety/social-media-minimum-age
82. eSafety Commissioner-Australian Government. (2023). *Roadmap for Age Verification.* https://www.esafety.gov.au/about-us/industry-regulation/social-media-age-restrictions
83. Australian Government. (2025). *Age Assurance Technology Trial: Final Report. Commonwealth of Australia.* https://ageassurance.com.au/report/
84. Segpay. (2024, August 20). *Mandatory age verification in Asia.* https://segpay.com/blog/mandatory-age-verification-asia/
85. Government of India, Ministry of Electronics and Information Technology. (2021). *The Information Technology Intermediary Guidelines and Digital Media Ethics Code.* https://www.meity.gov.in/static/uploads/2024/02/Information-Technology-Intermediary-Guidelines-and-Digital-Media-Ethics-Code-Rules-2021-updated-06.04.2023-.pdf
86. Government of Singapore. (2023). *Online Criminal Harms Act 2023.* https://sso.agc.gov.sg/Act/OCHA2023
87. Republic of Korea (2022). *Youth Protection Act-Ministry of Gender Equality and Family.* https://www.kimchang.com/en/insights/detail.kc?sch_section=4&idx=2547
88. Japan Today. (2026, April 22). *Japan eyes stricter age checks for young social media users.* https://japantoday.com/category/national/japan-eyes-stricter-age-checks-for-young-social-media-users
89. BBC News. (2026, February 3). *Spain plans to ban social media access for under-16s.* https://www.bbc.com/news/articles/c5y2nddvmryo
90. UNICEF. (2021). *Child online protection in South Africa.* https://www.unicef.org/southafrica

91. Biometric Update. (2026, April 1). *Malaysia's age verification rules for social media could be world's strictest.* https://www.biometricupdate.com/202604/malaysias-age-verification-rules-for-social-media-could-be-worlds-strictest
92. Age Verification Providers Association. (2025). *Standards and best practices for age verification.* https://avpassociation.com/standards-for-age-verification/
93. IEEE Standards Association. (2024). *IEEE Standard 2089.1-2024: IEEE standard for online age verification.* https://standards.ieee.org/ieee/2089.1/10700/
94. International Organization for Standardization. (2025). *ISO/IEC 27566-1:2025: Information security, cybersecurity and privacy protection – Age assurance systems – Part 1.* https://www.iso.org/obp/ui/en/#iso:std:iso-iec:27566:-1:ed-1:v1:en
95. Age Check Certification Scheme. (2021). *ACCS 2:2021: Data protection criteria for age assurance products.* https://ico.org.uk/for-organisations/advice-and-services/certification-schemes/certification-scheme-register/age-check-certification-scheme-accs/
96. European Commission. (2025). *Age verification blueprint (Version 2): Technical specifications for digital age verification systems.* https://digital-strategy.ec.europa.eu/en/news/commission-releases-enhanced-second-version-age-verification-blueprint
97. Digital Governance Standards Institute (DGSI). (2025). *CAN/DGSI 127: National standard for age assurance technologies.* https://dgc-cgn.org/new-national-standard-published-for-age-assurance-technologies/
98. Internet Society. (2025). *Policy brief: Age restrictions and online safety.* https://www.internetsociety.org/resources/policybriefs/2025/age-restrictions-and-online-safety/
99. UK Government. (2025). *Keeping children safe online: Changes to the Online Safety Act explained.* https://www.gov.uk/government/news/keeping-children-safe-online-changes-to-the-online-safety-act-explained
100. BBC News. (2025). *Online safety rules: Age checks for porn sites come into force.* https://www.bbc.com/news/articles/c1k81lj8nvpo
101. BBC News. (2025). *The top 3 cybersecurity risks posed by the Online Safety Act.* https://www.bbc.com/news/articles/cn72ydj70g5o

102. YouGov. (2026). *Eight months on, three quarters of Britons still support online age verification laws.* https://yougov.com/en-gb/articles/54405-eight-months-on-three-quarters-of-britons-still-support-online-age-verification-laws
103. BBC News. (2026). *Porn traffic drops after UK age checks, but VPN use rises.* https://www.bbc.com/news/articles/cgkz3m3re1zo
104. BBC News. (2026). *Pornhub to restrict UK access over age-verification rules.* https://www.bbc.com/news/articles/czr428rxg57o
105. Sky News. (2025). *Two-thirds of underage Australians still have access to social media despite ban, new research suggests.* https://news.sky.com/story/two-thirds-of-underage-australians-still-have-access-to-social-media-despite-ban-new-research-suggests-13531097
106. Prime Minister of Australia. (2026, January 16). *4.7 million accounts deactivated, removed or restricted.* https://www.pm.gov.au/media/4-7-million-accounts-deactivated-removed-or-restricted
107. UNICEF Australia. (2025). *After the ban: How young people are navigating social media now.* https://www.unicef.org.au/stories/after-the-ban-how-young-people-are-navigating-social-media-now
108. Liminal. (2025). *From pilot programs to global mandate: Age assurance's new reality.* https://liminal.co/articles/age-assurances-new-reality/
109. National Institute of Standards and Technology. (2024). *Face Analysis Technology Evaluation (FATE): Age estimation results.* https://nvlpubs.nist.gov/nistpubs/ir/2024/NIST.IR.8525.pdf
110. Bahari, M. H., McLaren, M., Van Leeuwen, D. A., & Van Hamme, H. (2014). *Age estimation from speech using i-vectors.* https://doi.org/10.21437/Interspeech.2014-321
111. Rémy, F., Saliba-Serre, B., Chaumoitre, K., Martrille, L., & Lalys, L. (2021). Age estimation from the biometric information of hand bones: Development of new formulas. *Forensic Science International*, 322, 110777. https://doi.org/10.1016/j.forsciint.2021.110777
112. Adib, A., Zhu, W.-P., & Ahmad, M. O. (2025). Age estimation via electrocardiogram from smartwatches. *npj Biomedical Innovations*, 2, Art. no. 35, 2025. https://www.nature.com/articles/s44385-025-00039-5

113. Biometric Update. (2025, November 21). *Aylo continues to argue site-level age verification is ineffective.* https://www.biometricupdate.com/202511/aylo-continues-to-argue-site-level-age-verification-is-ineffective
114. CityNews. (2025, November 25). *Meta pitching app store age verification law to Liberal government.* https://toronto.citynews.ca/2025/11/25/meta-pitching-app-store-age-verification-law-to-liberal-government/
115. Starc, V., & Schlegel, T. T. (2008). The effect of aging and cardiac disease on that portion of QT interval variability that is independent of heart rate variability. *Computers in Cardiology,* 2008, 315–317. https://ieeexplore.ieee.org/document/4749041
116. Erelund, S., Karp, K., Wiklund, U., Arvidsson, S., & Hörnsten, R. (2021). Are ECG changes in heart-healthy individuals of various ages related to cardiac disease 20 years later? *Upsala Journal of Medical Sciences,* 126(1), Article 6064. https://pubmed.ncbi.nlm.nih.gov/34349886/
117. Macfarlane, P. W. (2018). The influence of age and sex on the electrocardiogram. In P. L. M. Kerkhof & V. M. Miller (Eds.), *Sex-specific analysis of cardiovascular function* (pp. 93–106). Springer. https://pubmed.ncbi.nlm.nih.gov/30051379/
118. Attia, Z. I., Friedman, P. A., Noseworthy, P. A., Lopez-Jimenez, F., Ladewig, D. J., Satam, G., Pellikka, P. A., Munger, T. M., Asirvatham, S. J., Scott, C. G., Carter, R. E., & Kapa, S. (2019). Age and sex estimation using artificial intelligence from standard 12-lead ECGs. *Circulation: Arrhythmia and Electrophysiology,* 12(9), Article e007284. https://pubmed.ncbi.nlm.nih.gov/31450977/
119. Lima, E. M., Ribeiro, A. H., Paixão, G. M. M., Ribeiro, M. H., Pinto-Filho, M. M., Gomes, P. R., Oliveira, D. M., Sabino, E. C., Duncan, B. B., Giatti, L., Barreto, S. M., Meira, W., Jr., Schön, T. B., & Ribeiro, A. L. P. (2021). Deep neural network-estimated electrocardiographic age as a mortality predictor. *Nature Communications,* 12(1), Article 5117. https://doi.org/10.1038/s41467-021-25351-7
120. Lindow, T., Palencia-Lamela, I., Schlegel, T. T., & Ugander, M. (2022). Heart age estimated using explainable advanced electrocardiography. *Scientific Reports,* 12(1), Article 9840. https://doi.org/10.1038/s41598-022-13912-9

121. Ansari, M. Y., Qaraqe, M., Righetti, R., Serpedin, E., & Qaraqe, K. (2024). Enhancing ECG-based heart age: Impact of acquisition parameters and generalization strategies for varying signal morphologies and corruptions. *Frontiers in Cardiovascular Medicine,* 11, Article 1424585. https://doi.org/10.3389/fcvm.2024.1424585
122. Strodthoff, N., Wagner, P., Schaeffter, T., & Samek, W. (2021). Deep learning for ECG analysis: Benchmarks and insights from PTB-XL. *IEEE Journal of Biomedical and Health Informatics,* 25(5), 1519–1528. https://pubmed.ncbi.nlm.nih.gov/32903191/
123. Ball, R. L., Feiveson, A. H., Schlegel, T. T., Starc, V., & Dabney, A. R. (2014). Predicting "heart age" using electrocardiography. *Journal of Personalized Medicine,* 4(1), 65–78. https://doi.org/10.3390/jpm4010065
124. Adib, A., Zhu, W.-P., & Ahmad, M. O. (2025). *Smartwatch ECG age prediction.* GitHub. https://github.com/azfaradib/smart-watch-ecg-age-prediction
125. Adib, A., Zhu, W.-P., & Ahmad, M. O. (2022). *Adult and non-adult classification using ECG.* 2022 IEEE 7th Forum on Research and Technologies for Society and Industry Innovation (RTSI), pp. 174–179. https://doi.org/10.1109/RTSI55261.2022.9905194
126. Vaswani, A., Shazeer, N., Parmar, N., Uszkoreit, J., Jones, L., Gomez, A. N., Kaiser, Ł., & Polosukhin, I. (2017). Attention is all you need. In *Advances in Neural Information Processing Systems, Vol.* 30. https://arxiv.org/abs/1706.03762
127. Information Commissioner's Office. (n.d.). *Measurement of age assurance technologies.* https://ico.org.uk/for-organisations/uk-gdpr-guidance-and-resources/childrens-information/age-appropriate-design-code/measurement-of-age-assurance-technologies/
128. Yoti Ltd. (2023, December). *Yoti age estimation white paper.* https://www.yoti.com/wp-content/uploads/2023/12/Yoti-Age-Estimation-White-Paper-December-2023.pdf
129. Fitbit, Inc. (2022). *Fitbit Sense 2 user manual.* https://documents.4rgos.it/v1/static/1153705_R_D001documents.4rgos.it
130. Mozilla Foundation. (2021). *Fitbit Sense | Privacy & security guide.* https://www.mozillafoundation.org/en/privacynotincluded/fitbit-sense/

131. Xie, J., Zeng, J., Fu, F., Liu, H., & Liu, J. (2021). A signal quality assessment-based ECG waveform delineation method for wearable systems. *IEEE Journal of Biomedical and Health Informatics*, 25(7), 2571–2581. https://pubmed.ncbi.nlm.nih.gov/34432182/
132. Taji, B., & Zhang, P. (2019). *Signal quality assessment in wearable ECG devices.* University of Ottawa. https://ruor.uottawa.ca/items/952c41ca-33f8-45d6-bc33-602cbebc0b45

Index